Thorlák of Iceland

Who Rose Above Autism
to Become Patron Saint of his People

Written by

Aimee O'Connell

Illustrated by

Sigurbjorg Eyjolfsdottir

O'CONNELL

ISBN-13: 978-0990723141
ISBN-10: 0990723143

CHAOS TO ORDER PUBLISHING

San Jose, California

O'CONNELL

DEDICATION

To Bridget, whose smile is my treasure,
and who found St. Thorlák when we
needed him most.

ACKNOWLEDGEMENTS

I would like to extend my personal and heartfelt thanks to everyone who has offered their time, prayers and encouragement to me as I took on the most enjoyable challenge of bringing St. Thorlák's life to these pages. In particular, I wish to acknowledge:

> The Bishop, priests and religious of
> The Diocese of Reykjavik.
> Gunnar F. Guðmundsson.
> Eleanor Parker.
> Michael, my champion.
> Anne, my Secretary of the Interior.
> My Faithful Cheering Section.
> My "Roadie."

I add a warm smile and a nod to everyone else I have met along the path from Twenty First Century Rochester to Twelfth Century Skálholt.
In the words of Bishop Thorlák: "*I have always been capable of little, if others have not helped me.*"

Thank you.

O'CONNELL

CONTENTS

O'CONNELL

O'CONNELL

WWW.C2OP.COM

O'CONNELL

PUBLISHER'S FOREWORD

The skyline of west Reykjavik is dominated by a sturdy looking Gothic structure set on a hill. It is known as *Landakotskirkja* or The Cathedral of Christ the King. Dedicated in 1929, it is the seat of the Catholic Church in Iceland. Within its walls lay many interesting items: Over the high altar a statue of Christ standing on top of the world, carved from cedar it is unique because its artist, Campanya, gave explicit instructions that no copy was ever to be made. A medieval wooden statue of the Holy Mother and Child believed to be from the fourteenth century. It was crowned by Pope John Paul II upon his pastoral visit to Iceland in 1989.

Near the entrance, along a somewhat nondescript white wall, is a rather straightforward, almost stern, looking statue. It is of the twelfth century bishop Thorlák Thórhallsson. Thorlák was officially declared "The Patron Saint of Iceland" by Pope John Paul II on January 14, 1984. However, Icelanders had already, informally, declared him to be so some eight centuries earlier.

Yet Thorlák hardly seems well celebrated today. Perhaps this is because Iceland has only a small Catholic population. However, this was not always the case for in Thorlák's day all of Iceland was

Catholic by decree. And even when the Protestant Reformation came to Iceland in, 1550 AD, the last Catholic bishop of Iceland, Jón Arason, refused to give up the faith even at the point of a sword. Later, Jon Sveinsson writes in his <u>A Journey Across Iceland</u> of how the Lutheran bishops of his day would wear a special vestment, given by the Pope to Jón Arason, whenever ordaining their own clergy. And this effort to maintain a real and tangible connection to the Catholic past of Iceland went on, at least, until the dawn of the twentieth century.

Since there seems to have remained a general fervor for the Catholic faith down through the ages in Iceland the relative anonymity of its patron saint still must be explained. Perhaps it is because that even among the great story telling people of Iceland, with their wonderful traditions of sagas and extensive family genealogies, the complete story of Thorlák has still never been told? And here we come to one of the primary reasons for this current work. Yet, as Thorlák was a man of many layers, the reasons for now telling his story may be of many layers as well.

Recent reports from Iceland with regard to Down syndrome pregnancy screening were disturbing. However, these reports failed to take into account the many good things Icelanders have long done for people with special needs. The Sólheimar Ecovillage was founded in 1930. The heart of their ideology is to give all persons a fair chance in life by focusing on their possibilities rather than their limitations. Sólheimar aims to create the space for each resident to take every opportunity which arises to grow and develop. Versatility is the strength of Sólheimar so people with special needs who reside there are always at the centre of the community. This works through the process of reverse integration: Those without special needs adapt to the abilities of those with special needs and then all work together to make their community one of an equal and sustainable nature. In this way Sólheimar serves as a model for how to treat people with special needs not just in Iceland, but in the world.

So we see today in Iceland, as in the world, a debate going on about people with special needs. Do we want to use science and technology to eliminate these people, or do we want to accept all persons as they are created and find caring and innovative ways to integrate them into human community?

Another question that should be raised here is whether Autism is really a special need or, perhaps, more of a special ability? Josef Pieper writes in his book Leisure: The Basis of Culture of how modern thought has lost the essential aspect of contemplation with the human effort of *ratio* or reason having almost entirely supplanted the divine gift of *intellectus* or intellectual vision. Indeed, Pieper's thesis suggests that the contemplative abilities which many we label as autistic display are perhaps the essential missing ingredient in most of modern thought.

Now into this debate steps Thorlák. As if divine providence itself had been waiting through the ages for the right moment in time for his story to be fully told. His is not just a story of history but of human dignity. For if to become a Saint Thorlák had to overcome a special need then special needs are, in fact, a part of the very process of human sanctification! Not just in terms of the individual but, also, in terms of how human community itself might be sanctified through the placing of people with special needs at its very centre.

Thus we are proud to present the story of Thorlák of Iceland. A man who overcame great struggles to speak to his own age, and perhaps has much more to say to our own.

John C. Wilhelmsson

CHAPTER ONE

THE BIRTH OF THORLÁK

The wind is always present, whether hovering over
the sea in waiting or unleashing its playful abandon
on land, chasing snow around outcroppings or
racing itself across the plain. There are none
unfamiliar with the wind in Iceland, for to call that
land home demands a readiness to withstand
sudden buffets of resistance at a moment's notice.
The intrepid spirit passed down by Iceland's first
settlers imbues her people with respect, even
cautious admiration for the wind as a fierce but
fickle ally. The truly robust of heart are those few
who genuinely love this wild wind of the North
Atlantic – who, stretching their arms to catch the
fullness of its roar, exhilarate in surrendering to
something beyond our reach, connecting to a power
far above our sight, and feeling its reciprocal
embrace.

Lit by a sun reluctant to set, the wind of the spring
and summer months whistles and sings as it rolls
and teases the Icelandic terrain. In stark contrast,
the midwinter wind is more of a stern governess
shushing the farmland over blankets of dormancy.

In the year 1133, in the district of Fljótshlíð, southern Iceland, under a snow-packed turf roof at the farmstead called Hlíðarendi , the February wind took backstage as Halla, wife of the merchant fisherman Thórhall, labored and gave birth to their son Thorlák. Thórhall and his family were known as faithful, good-living people. Thórhall's son would gain a reputation for having unusual wisdom and presence of mind as a very young boy. He was seldom seen playing with the other children, but instead seemed to spend his days thinking, pondering… and laughing with uncontrollable joy each time the exuberant Icelandic wind found in him an eager playmate.

Commonly found among Norse families even today, the name *Thorlák* has as its root the notorious god of thunder, Thor. The Norse element *–Lák* means both "contends with" and "playful." The connotation is not so much sporting as it is cunning: a playful contender, whose hope of victory has the advantage of confidence over provoked anger. Surely, one who finds joy in the severe Icelandic wind would be a direct challenge to one who relies on thunder to intimidate. However Providential his naming, Thorlák Thórhallsson would be recorded in Iceland's history as one who withstood the most severe resistance with the stalwart strength of his own vulnerability.

CHAPTER TWO

THORLÁK'S *CHILDHOOD*

The family of Halla Steinadottir and Thórhall Thorláksson was like most other families in twelfth century Iceland. They had three children: Thorlák, born in 1133; and two sisters, Ragnheið (ca. 1135) and Eyvǫr (ca. 1137). Their life centered around farm labor, as the southern coast of Iceland is home to the most favorable land for crop farming and raising livestock. Farms do exist in the other regions of Iceland, but the soil quality varies greatly as does climatic conditions. Southern Iceland in the twelfth century produced rye, barley and root vegetables, as well as abundant grass for the sheep, goats, horses and cattle to graze upon.

Iceland, being an island roughly the land size of Austria or America's state of Kentucky, is practically its own complete world, having farmland, mountains, lava fields, glaciers, hot springs and black sand beaches all within its approximately 1400 km (870 mile) perimeter. The southern region alone boasts three glaciers, four volcanoes and a crater field, variegated throughout by numerous hot springs and rivers. The southern shore is a rich

contrast of black-sand beaches and imposing rock
formations. Some of Iceland's most beautiful
waterfalls are found in the south, including
Seljalandsfoss, Gullfoss and Skógafoss, each flanked
by soaring basalt cliffs. The names of these
waterfalls are tourist destinations today, but in
Thorlák's day, the world knew little of Iceland or its
remarkable natural majesty. In turn, those born
there knew little of the world far beyond Iceland's
shores. It is no surprise to imagine how such
natural splendor, extraordinary to most of us, would
foster a deep and lifelong sense of contemplative
wonder in those for whom it was their ordinary
setting.

Along with farming, Icelanders of the twelfth
century dealt heavily in fishing and the seafaring
trades. Thórhall was a successful seafarer merchant
before he married and established his household.
Icelandic merchants harvested and traded ivory
from walrus and narwhal tusks, although it was
much more common to deal in the more easily
obtainable commodities, such as wool and cloth.
Whale bones, dried cod and sulfur were other
goods offered abroad by Icelandic merchants. Most
merchants were also farmers by necessity, as there

was no distinction between the two, since growing
seasons were so short and livestock in limited
supply. Each activity supplied, and supplemented,
the other. When harsh weather went on for
prolonged periods, both farming and trade suffered
great losses.

Young Thorlák grew up in the most lush and varied
stretch of Iceland's southern countryside, where
summers were warm and winters snowy. He was
about 23km (14 miles) inland from the sea. A short
walk to the east would bring him to Gluggafoss, the
waterfall that cascades through "windows" in the
rock formations. Summers became endless
meadows of romping and wandering when the sun
just barely dips below the horizon even at midnight,
but then autumn and winter supplied the long
stretches of darkness to study the constellations and
witness the heavenly dance of the aurora borealis.
He often dwelled in his imagination studying the
stars and contemplating the heavens. Thorlák
embraced astronomy as the son of a seafarer who
mystically relied on the precision of the stars for
accuracy in direction. His father told stories of the
Irish Saint Brendan the Navigator which captivated
him every time as he tried to imagine a land so

green compared to the yellow-hued grasses and black-gray basalt of Iceland's outcroppings. The unseen took life as he contemplated the boundless nighttime skies, wakefully dreaming of the open seas and envisioning the wind catching him as it does the sails of ships, carrying him firmly and swiftly to places beyond his ability to imagine.

Thorlák loved stories. He listened intently to anyone weaving a tale of character and suspense, whether genealogical saga or cautionary myth. He persistently asked questions of his storytellers, seeking the tiniest details, homing in on each character as though it were his duty to understand their very souls. He wished his playmates would speak of great things and great characters, but they had little patience for the depth and detail of his imagination. He found much more pleasure in grabbing the attention of the adults who came and went about the farmstead, and many became quite fond of their precocious young inquisitor. The adults took extra time to speak with Thorlák, asking as many questions of him, it seems, as he proposed to them. When they dismissed him, he was rarely seen with other children, preferring to contemplate off by himself until he was called back home.

Thorlák was a sweet child, eager to please his parents and delighted when they showed him affection. There was no better storyteller than his own mother, and nothing was more comforting than listening to her recite the genealogy of her family. Thorlák often found it difficult to sleep during the night, particularly when awakening from loud sounds or the many detailed dreams he had, and he would seek out his mother to comfort him with tales of her childhood and memories of relatives. He found he could ease back into sleep as he imagined what his forebears might have looked like, perhaps with darker hair and softer faces than those set like the hardy Norsemen determined to conquer the formidable Icelandic terrain.

Books were rare in any household at that time, and few children received much in the way of education. Work around the farmstead was a constant occupation for all ages. A Latin Psalter was kept at hand, read occasionally by the adults, silently and aloud. To Thorlák, printed script was a wonder to behold. Each line contained patterns he slowly came to recognize as he traced the letters and tried to recall their recitation. Before he turned six, Thorlák had deciphered and committed the entire

Psalter to memory. The very first psalm in that book was not only his first triumph of decoding the mystery of reading, but also spoke deeply to his heart as he considered each word and what it meant.

> *Blessed is the one*
> *who does not walk in step with the wicked*
> *or stand in the way that sinners take*
> *or sit in the company of mockers,*
> *but whose delight is in the law of the Lord,*
> *and who meditates on his law day and night.*
> *That person is like a tree planted by streams of water,*
> *which yields its fruit in season*
> *and whose leaf does not wither—*
> *whatever they do prospers.*
> *Not so the wicked!*
> *They are like chaff*
> *that the wind blows away.*
> *Therefore the wicked will not stand in the judgment,*
> *nor sinners in the assembly of the righteous.*
> *For the Lord watches over the way of the righteous, but*
> *the way of the wicked leads to destruction.*
> *Psalm One*

Every time Thorlák opened the Psalter, he re-read Psalm One, adopting the poet's words as a prayer he would recite from memory as he wandered the Icelandic countryside. He considered the words as he listened to the stories of men and women, searching out parables in each tale, coming quickly to understand that God in Heaven has a definite order for people to follow. When people live in humble appreciation of God and one another, abundance flows. When people turn against each other and compete so as to unfairly wield power over what God intended for everyone to have… ambition becomes corruption. The concepts were lofty for a five year old, yet he grasped them with simple perfection.

The further Thorlák read in the Psalter, the more interested he became in human nature and God's order, and the more he wished to discuss this with the adults. Not only did he seek out adults to talk to him, but now he looked for adults who were comfortable discussing Scripture and matters of theology. His parents received many comments about his unusual behavior. For his part, he may have been unusual, but he was not a difficult child. He was easy going, cheerful and diligent in nearly everything asked of him – including being ushered back toward the other children as the adults needed to get back to work.

In twelfth-century Iceland, just as anywhere else across the plains of time, climatic conditions determined the fate of the economy and the geographical centers of power. A severe year of weather in the early 1140s devastated merchants and fishermen who were unable to sail. Crops and livestock suffered along with those who tended them. Many families found themselves destitute through no fault of their own. Desperate parents were forced to break up their households and foster children in other families when provisions ran out. Thórhall and Halla found themselves in dire straits when Thorlák was nine. Halla, known for her resourcefulness, approached the crisis with strategic calculation. Their family had distant connections to the Oddaverjar, the wealthy clan who owned the farm estate, church and learning center at Oddi in Rangárvellir. At Oddi resided several priests and citizens of prominent descent. Besides being a thriving farmstead, Oddi was also a prestigious school for promising young men. Halla, banking on Thorlák's notoriety as a child prodigy, approached the Oddaverjar with the proposition that he be taken in and educated there in exchange for Halla and two of her daughters offering themselves as servants. Thórhall would go his own way to try and recover anything he could of his livelihood.

Fatefully, this arrangement was found acceptable. Thórhall divided his holdings and left to seek prosperity elsewhere. Thorlák and his two sisters, Ragnheið and Eyvǫr, moved westward with their mother to Rangárvellir to begin anew at making a go of Icelandic living.

CHAPTER THREE

STUDY AT ODDI

As if by Divine Providence, Thorlák's childhood home was in relatively close proximity to Iceland's singular center of culture and learning. Oddi was not simply a boarding school or an outgrowth of a monastery. Oddi was a community formed by the learned and holy men of the Oddaverjar clan, beginning back with the legendary priest Sæmundur Fróði in the late eleventh century. There are many fantastic stories of Sæmundur "The Learned" traveling from Iceland to Franconia, on the European continent, to study philosophy and spirituality from the leading minds there. Legend claims he was strongly persuaded to become a master of *galdur*, the dark arts of sorcery, as the Devil himself saw Sæmundur would be a prized pupil. Sæmundur resisted, maintaining his allegiance to the Christian faith. He is said to have been challenged by the Devil in various forms on several occasions and deftly eluded him each time. Sæmundur's final encounter found Satan in the form of a seal who offered him passage to Iceland from France on his back. Legend says he agreed, knowing fully well it was his adversary who would demand allegiance when they arrived. As they approached the southern Iceland shore, Sæmundur struck the seal decisively on the head with his Holy Bible and proclaimed his title as a priest of the One, True God. It was thus that Oddi was established as a Christian, not pagan, institution. This was said to have happened in 1078 – just barely one generation after the Icelandic nation first adopted Christianity by declaring pagan worship unlawful. In actuality, many people still held pagan sentiments even as Christian practices were taking root.

Sæmundur the Priest had two sons, Eyjólfur and Loft, who were the premiere scholars and power brokers at Oddi. Loft became a chieftain and married Þora Magnúsdatter – better known as the daughter of King Magnús "Barelegs" III of Norway. They had a son, Jón, who was a top student at Oddi and protégé of the growing Oddaverjar clan.

Eyjólfur Sæmundsson followed his father's footsteps to the priesthood and taught theology and philosophy to the boys who came to study at Oddi. It was he who took in young Thorlák, and in fact was very fond of him. Thorlák referred to Eyjólfur as his foster-father, a connection he felt sincerely.

When Thorlák came to live at Oddi, he found it
both daunting in size and exciting in prospect.
There were books here and learned men with whom
to discuss them. There were studious young men
training for the priesthood as well as ambitious
youth refining the oratorical and political skills that
would put them among the ranks of the *goðar*,
Iceland's chieftains. The Oddaverjar had strong
influence among the clans in Iceland, and their
patronage practically guaranteed advancement in
Iceland's social structure.

While Thorlák lived as a student there, Ragnheið
and Eyvǫr studied the domestic arts with the other
girls. They made cheese from the sheep they
milked; they also sheared them to spin wool and
weave cloth. Girls also mended clothing and
maintained the sails for the men's ships. They
performed the ordinary household cleaning and
chores, and they tended to the needs of those who
were older or infirm. Thorlák's sisters were in good
company with the other girls and young women
there, and they found their lives quite suitable in
this new home. Ragnheið was prompt to
distinguish herself from among the others and soon
made the acquaintance of Jón, the eighteen-year-old

grandson of King Magnús Barelegs – who found her engaging eyes and quick wit quite winsome.

Thorlák was at once awed and overwhelmed by this abrupt change in everything he knew his life to be. Books, education and learned men guiding him were privileges he had never expected, and the setting felt foreign and intimidating. He was used to having others around him, but he normally kept to himself, saving for when he found a passing merchant or farmer to tell him a story or answer his questions. Being in a school was entirely different. No more could he simply ponder in the forum of his mind. Here, he was expected to attend to studies prescribed by his elders and then to discuss his thoughts in formal, organized fashion. Reciting answers on request was far different from wandering with notions in silence, and the task was daunting. Thorlák often found himself unable to speak, even as he tried with earnest effort and intent. When he began his response, he felt a rush of words tangle somewhere between his mind and his chest, tightening his throat and pulling his face into a scowl of frustration. His eyes glancing at his classmates, his breath drawn in determination, and his jaw set, he discordantly stumbled over syllables when he held his head high to enunciate for the entire group. He found he was better able to speak his thoughts completely with his eyes cast down, his chin close to his chest, and his voice reined in to a low mumble. In stark contrast, Thorlák excelled in writing. Compositions and essays, eloquent and thought-provoking, came easily to him, as did poetry. His instructors saw no gap in his aptitude despite his awkward speaking style and presumed it was a matter of developing confidence. One on one, his mentors gently pushed him toward better diction and presentation. His teachers were priests who had studied abroad and recognized both the depth of his insight and the potential for great academic advancement. His remarkable wisdom and devout love of spirituality already set him apart from his peers, and so his instructors did not feel he was so much "different" as he was an exceptionally gifted student.

As advantageous a place as Oddi was to a precocious child-philosopher like Thorlák, his greatest joy was going off by himself to let his thoughts soar, uncontained as the updrafts of the North Atlantic wind. He grasped theology with great depth and breadth, which lifted his thoughts ever closer to God. Despite the idealness of his setting, he secretly felt terrified that he could no longer be a child. His teachers were kind-hearted mentors who failed to see that he was still a boy beneath the prodigy. They never saw the yawning emotional needs of a child acutely aware that his father was gone. His mother was not far, but was no longer living in the quarters where he stayed. He ached, too, with the loss of his mother's doting. Though wise beyond his years, he was a child of nine with no fewer fears than any young boy wanting the reassurance that everything will be okay. He learned in his first few months at Oddi to hide his needs, particularly when he would awaken with a start, disoriented and terrified by frightening dreams, but out of the reach of his mother's soothing – indeed, under a completely different roof. He muffled his night terrors and cried in secret, spending wakeful nights seeking solace in the constellations he recognized, reminding himself that the firmament endures no matter what we cannot control in our own lives.

Thorlák called Oddi his home for the next six years. He was extremely well liked by everyone there and was top among students in nearly every aspect of

his education. He retained his peculiar habit of
mumbling when he spoke, but now and again he
would become caught up in great enthusiasm over
one topic or another, in study or in leisure, and
would show an exuberant zeal that projected his
voice with ease, and at length. He rarely sought out
others in debate, but he did not shrink from the
opportunity to express his opinion on whatever
matter might have come up in discussion. Still,
Thorlák was the best at listening and observing,
which won the affection of many who enjoyed
having a forum in which to speak without
interruption.

Thorlák's mentors assumed his path would be one
of clerical ordination. It seemed unfathomable that
someone of his wisdom and spiritual depth could
live any other life, particularly in a country still
considered backwards by their European peers for
its reliance on farming and fishing. They believed
Thorlák would leave Iceland for higher pursuits,
and his extended family championed this idea
whole-heartedly. In his father's absence, Thorlák
would look after the welfare of his mother and
sisters. Perhaps he could establish himself abroad
and send for his family, or at least amass enough

success through political connections to provide for their security and comfort in Iceland.

When he was fourteen, Thorlák's mentors began preparing him for ordination as a deacon. It was unprecedented for someone this young, but everyone agreed he was academically ready, and likewise, his even-temperedness set him apart in precocious maturity. He was said to be better suited for Holy Orders than many older adults seeking this office. Thorlák accepted this course as he had everything else — with gratitude, congeniality and much introspection. His mother was especially vocal with her praise.

As he turned these plans over and over in his mind, Thorlák became increasingly aware of his role and responsibility in the story unfolding. His life thus far had been spent studying the lives of others, their stories, and the lessons of their achievements. He began to feel the magnitude of what lie ahead, and he felt a sense of awe. What a marvelous life about to open up to him! What a magnificent realization, to be found worthy of God's call! What accomplishment, to see his teachers and his mother and kinsfolk looking upon him with such pride, such pleasure! He did very well by them indeed, and he contemplated the far-reaching implications of the future ahead.

He experienced, for the first time in his life, a horrible sense of doubt. His mentors saw a great man to come. He saw himself as a child, small, and scared. He worried he had fooled everyone into thinking he was stronger and more capable than he was... or, perhaps, he had fooled himself.

As always when he felt anxious, Thorlák went quietly off by himself, outdoors, standing at the stone garden wall and gazing up into the heavens. He saw the openness, the endlessness of the sky, and felt it fixed upon his shoulders as a yoke, impossible to bear. He recalled his earliest memories, when his mother and father kept house while he and his sisters played, and had a most unsettling thought: What if that was the greater embodiment of God's plan for men and women? Are not ordinary people, who labor diligently for their livelihood, in the greater position to glorify God than those handed privilege? Philosophy and theology were important, to be sure, but to abandon ordinary labor in their pursuit seemed an unfair burden on the ones he was said to be serving. Furthermore, if he could truly name that which would make him happiest, it would be to experience the fullness of childhood – not enter into the political entanglements of adulthood. He wondered if he was meant to be a father, a *húsbóndi*, distributing these great spiritual riches to a home filled with children rather than doling them out as a parish priest.

Thorlák's angst gave way to sorrow. He struggled to admit the thoughts he was entertaining, and then began to worry he had not chosen this life for himself. Everything thus far had been handed to him, expected of him, and lauded by those pleased with his compliance. The specter of doubt grew larger and colder as he wondered if these thoughts were sincere, or if they were a surge of his own will, a latent rebelliousness, an unknown cache of resentment which must be vanquished before bringing perdition to his soul.

The youthful teen wrestled his mind without resolution. He thought to pray but could not find the courage to face his own disobedience.

As he stood, alone and fearful, he felt himself swept up in a warmth like that of the sweetest memory of his mother's gentle embrace, reassuring him that

God has been with us since the beginning of time, is with us now, and remains with us long past even the moment we lose sight of him over the horizon. God orders all. Our destiny is sanctified if we hand it over to Him and trust that His designs are far more loving than anything we could try to imagine.

Thorlák could feel and smell his childhood even more fully than if he was transported back in time. *"Móðir…"* he found himself whispering aloud, and then caught himself. His mother was asleep with the others in her quarters. Yet, he felt a soothing touch, as though in his very soul. The words came into his mind: *Son, behold thy Mother.*

"Heil sért þú, María!" he exclaimed in a whisper, and in a way he could not explain with words, he sensed someone's smile. He knew that the Blessed Virgin Mary, Mother of Jesus, must have heard his plea and was now there as his own mother in his moment of littleness. He paused for a moment, in a state somewhere between imagination and reality, but then wondered if that was not what authentic prayer really was. He let go of his hesitation and permitted himself to imagine the embrace, and to speak earnestly, as a young boy in his mother's lap, about his fears and hopes and yearnings.

Anyone passing by would have seen only a teenage boy gazing at the stars with eyes half closed and dreamy smile. Thorlák paid no mind. He spoke nothing out loud, but for the rest of that night, he conversed in his heart with the Blessed Mother, finding great encouragement and wisdom in her presence. By daybreak, he was at ease with the prospect that God had intentions for him that could only be fulfilled if he followed the clerical vocation. His yearning for children would not go unheard. His bride might not come to him in the style imagined by those contracting marriage, but he was assured he would somehow live out every wish of his heart.

Thorlák's experience empowered him in ways that would only be revealed as he recalled that night for years to come. The next day, he picked up his studies dutifully, and when he was fifteen, he received ordination as a Deacon of the Church.

O'CONNELL

CHAPTER FOUR

DEACON TO PRIEST

Deacon Thorlák was beloved by everyone who recognized him in his district as the inquisitive boy from the farmstead. He was an endearing apprentice to the parish priests, assisting them in their duties and observing everything carefully as far as the day to day management and operations of their offices. He took great care to get to know the families in the parish. Even if he recognized them by name, he took the time to know each person's story, listening carefully and pondering them as well as if each were a book of philosophy. He was always fond of the children in his parishes and sat listening to them whenever he could.

Of all his clerical duties, Thorlák relished assisting with baptisms. To him, it was no mere ritual; Thorlák felt as much awe as though he stood witnessing an actual birth. First, the baby was brought inside the church and presented to the priest by its father. Often, kinsfolk accompanied them, along with the child's Godparents. Thorlák helped the priest dab a finger of sea salt into the baby's mouth as a gesture of bestowing wisdom.

The priest prayed over the child and the baptismal party recited the prayers of the church together: the *Our Father,* the *Hail Mary* and the *Credo.* At last, the baby was immersed in the font. As the priest anointed the child in the name of the Father, and of the Son, and of the Holy Spirit, Thorlák felt the life of grace approach the soul before him. He could almost see it, for a fleeting moment, and sensed a power enter the air surrounding them before being drawn into the nose and mouth of the gasping child, its tiny lungs filling with the *ruah* of God Himself. Each and every baptism left Thorlák in a state of deep and reverent joy.

Thorlák continued his studies in theology as he performed the duties of a Deacon, concentrating now on learning matters of finance and trade, property management and wealth. The churches in Iceland at that time were privately owned by the farmsteaders who erected them on their own property. These churches generated income for the farm through contributions collected from the faithful in the district, and in turn were maintained by all on the farmstead. Erecting a church was a wise investment monetarily and socially, and ordinary citizens gained good political favor

through such alliances. Thorlák closely observed
the interplay of social, economic and political
dynamics. He had a good measure of his mother's
thrift and instinctive knack for negotiation. His
mentors were quite pleased and made note of his
proficiencies in all of these areas.

The scholarly young deacon divided his time
between assisting the priests, praying, writing and
reading. When he was not in study, he greatly
enjoyed keeping company with his mother, who
regaled him with facts and fascinations from
Icelandic genealogy. Not only did each family keep
a meticulous genealogy for themselves, but the
entire Icelandic people were excellent historians,
and Halla was an excellent storyteller. She still
captivated Thorlák with vivid tales of his ancestors,
far and near, savoring each twist and surprise as
though it was her first time telling them. One of his
favorites drew from the *Flóamanna Saga*, a well-
known story of early settlers from the tenth and
eleventh centuries. The Saga's hero, Thorgils, was a
companion of Erik the Red during the exploration
and settlement of Greenland. He was also one of
the first Icelanders to embrace Christianity by
renouncing the pagan gods in a public baptism.

Thorgils' story included countless travels, adventures and perils between Norway, Scotland, Ireland, Greenland and Iceland. He miraculously raised his infant son on his own after his wife was killed en route to Greenland. The *Flóamanna Saga* told of many encounters with demonic adversaries, including the mighty Thor himself who mercilessly harassed Thorgils for publicly denying the heathen gods. Near the end of his life, Thorgils married a woman named Helga. They had a daughter Jórunn,

who grew, married, and had a daughter Eyvǫr.

Eyvǫr grew and married Thorlák, and they had a son, Thórhall. This Thórhall became Halla's husband: the fisherman-merchant-farmer who departed from his family six years prior, and was still greatly missed by his son the deacon. Thorlák slowly traced up the bloodline in his mind, feeling the strong bond between himself, his kinsmen and their namesakes. He and his sister were the Thorlák and Eyvǫr of his generation, and he felt proud to carry on his family's pledge of Christianity made by his great-great-grandfather.

Djákna Thorlák felt the great shock that went through the Diocese of Skálholt in late September,

1148. On the Feast of St. Michael, Bishop Magnús Einarsson died unexpectedly in a terrible fire along with eight other priests, leaving everyone stunned and Skálholt without a bishop. Iceland, though sparsely populated, had been divided into two Dioceses by the Archbishop of Niðaros, Norway in 1106. It was a very practical solution for Icelanders, who were naturally split between North and South by the glaciers and volcanic mountains which made it impossible to traverse the country through the middle. By forming a Diocese with its own Bishop in the south and west (Skálholt) and retaining the existing Diocese solely in the north (Hólar), the Church could more regularly carry out its duties without placing demands of perilous travel on its leaders.

The Diocese of Skálholt quickly felt the loss of their bishop: there could be no ordinations, no consecration of new church buildings, no leadership among the clerics — and, nobody to collect money for the treasury. The decline in revenue prompted the loudest calls for a new bishop, as Bishop Björn Gilsson of Hólar could not be expected to oversee this duty or to visit Skálholt with any regularity. The past two Bishops of Skálholt came from the

Haukdælir clan, one of the six predominant families in Iceland. Now, the Haukdælir named another of their chieftains, Hall Teitsson, to assume the vacant bishop's seat. A short time after his nomination, and before he could be consecrated, Hall, too, died unexpectedly. The succession passed to Hall's son, Gizur – but he was traveling abroad at the time it happened, and was unable to return in a timely manner to be consecrated and assume the seat.

These unusual delays found Skálholt without a Bishop for more than a year. To offer some relief, in 1151, Bishop Björn of Hólar made the trip south for a brief pastoral visit. He waived the usual period of scrutiny given to candidates for the priesthood and ordained a large gathering of eligible men in one mass ceremony. Bishop Björn would finally name the next Bishop of Skálholt, Klæng Thorsteinsson, who was consecrated the following year. Gizur Hallsson, meanwhile, became a powerful Icelandic chieftain instead of a bishop, but he did not let go of his clerical interests completely. For the rest of his career, Gizur kept an unofficial stance as an influential political advisor to the Diocese of Skálholt.

Included among the large group of candidates ordained by Bishop Björn was the eighteen-year-old deacon from Oddi. Everyone present recognized Thorlák's youth as testimony to his reputation, since those standing with him were substantially older. As with his previous milestones, Thorlák accepted his ordination with humility and gratitude. He still wondered at how he had earned such remarkable privilege but did not waver in his confidence as he had in secret four years earlier. He trusted that he was not simply being advanced out of political favor even if he had the backing of one of Iceland's powerful clans. He instinctively felt himself becoming each day a little more of the person God imagined him to be.

Father Thorlák Thórhallsson was now a fully vested priest in the Church. He diligently worked to see how he would best be able to serve the people in his district by closely observing the duties and specialties of the other clerics in Skálholt's diocese. He took great care in everything he did, down to the smallest detail, making sure he left nothing undone at the end of the day. The parishes he oversaw may have been small, but he approached them with the same diligence he might have shown to the greatest cathedral. Consequently, his parishes were notably well-managed and prosperous.

Séra Thorlák's popularity with his parishioners was just as strong as it had been in his days as deacon. His demeanor was thoughtful and gentle, and everyone who sought his counsel found him wise well beyond his youth. His virtue drew many to him, and many more to follow his example.

Besides being younger, Thorlák stood out in the way he approached his vocation. He strictly held to his daily habit of prayer, pondering verses of Sacred Scripture as the first and foremost guide to approaching his work. He found it energizing to read a particular psalm, or an epistle of St. Paul, or an exhortation from the Gospels, and then turn it over and over in his mind as he conducted the ordinary affairs of his office. It excited him to see the teachings of Jesus come to life in his daily routine. To his great disappointment, many of his fellow priests disregarded his approach as naïve and inexperienced. Some even called him a child, suggesting he was more like a boy pretending to be a priest than a man who comprehended the ways of the world. In their minds, his love of reading belonged with the highbrows on the European continent who were completely oblivious to the real man's labor found among the hardy farmsteaders and fishermen of the north. Most priests did not, as Thorlák had imagined, sit together in fellowship to discuss the depth and application of the Gospels.

In feeling separated from his colleagues, Séra Thorlák mused that the clergy in Iceland rarely considered their vocations as the fulfillment of the Kingdom of God. Rather, their ambitions pointed them toward fortifying the domains of their own provisions and comfort. In fact, most priests seemed indistinguishable from any other men, save for their clerical dress and political privilege. Priests were frequent guests of important people, plied with favors and gifts by prosperous merchants and householders, and guaranteed steady supplies of food, drink and entertainment. Several were proudly married, and several more kept concubines and mistresses. Priests boasted whenever they fathered sons, legitimately within or illegitimately outside of their marriages, as sons would carry on the priestly bloodline.

On a deep level, Thorlák knew the priesthood was meant for far greater spiritual achievements than were being realized in Iceland. It troubled his heart to find so few genuine students of Christianity among his fellow clerics. He began writing his musings and Scriptural reflections in private journals. He found the best audience for his thoughts consisted of the farmers and fishermen and laborers in his district – just as he found when he was a young boy. In turn, these, the most ordinary of people, just as greatly edified him as he might have imparted wisdom to them.

This yearning for deeper spiritual study would not go unrewarded. As also had been the case in his childhood, the right people noticed Thorlák's love of theological study and aspiration toward a more meaningful priesthood. His mentors at Oddi would once more provide him the way forward.

O'CONNELL

CHAPTER FIVE

STUDY ABROAD

With the priests in his district dismissing theology as something best kept in books, Thorlák happily found it dwelling among the least educated people. However, his patrons from the School at Oddi felt his academic gifts could do much more for Iceland – and for them – than being scattered about the countryside. Thus, in 1153, Thorlák was approached by his mentors from the Oddaverjar clan with the proposition of traveling to the European continent to study with hopes of securing both his allegiance, and their further interests.

The Oddaverjar clan held strong social power in central and southern Iceland throughout the 12th century. Through grand philanthropic gestures and association with European intelligentsia, they gained abundant political connections at home and abroad. It was little surprise they singled their star pupil out from among the clergy to offer him the opportunity to study in continental Europe, and Thorlák eagerly accepted the honor. His mother and sisters were overjoyed at this privilege and further alliance with such a prominent clan.

As it happened, a much stronger alliance had already begun between Thorlák's family and the Oddaverjar clan, though under less felicitous circumstances.

Jón Loftsson, a promising member of the Oddaverjar family, although somewhat older than Thorlák was educated alongside him year by year. Jón was not only the grandson of Sæmundur Froði on his father's side, but on his mother's side was the grandson of King Magnús III of Norway. Being of princely lineage, Jon Loftsson was naturally steered into a political career, and would eventually become one of Iceland's most powerful chieftains. His impressive genealogy granted him both political connections straight from birth and the best teachers anyone could have in Iceland at that time.

Jón was deeply infatuated with Ragnheið, Thorlák's sister. Jón and Ragnheið gravitated toward one another from the day she arrived at Oddi – she, a child of seven, and he, and a man of eighteen. They developed an unspoken bond between them, sending playful signals with their eyes whenever they passed one another and seeking out each other's company frequently. As Ragnheið matured, it became difficult to tell which of the two charmed the other with greater flirtation. Although the two were inseparable, Jón's family had clear plans for his future that did not include Ragnheið. Marriage propositions were made for mutual gain, and Ragnheið, after all, was a servant on the estate with no holdings. Jón was matched instead with a woman from a more suitable family, Halldóra Brandsdottir, and the two were married around 1150.

Nonetheless, Jón and Ragnheið remained a pair, doing little to hide their affections even as Halldóra gave birth to her first daughter with Jón. At the time, mistresses were an acceptable sort of scandal; improper, but seldom discouraged. Political leaders had concubines if they so desired, and few were wont to challenge them. Extramarital affairs were commonplace among the ordinary people just the same, and challenging the morals of the chieftains would call into account the habits of all of those who preferred to take liberties from the bonds of matrimony. It was easier to accept illicit relationships than to try and curtail the ones already in progress.

There is little doubt that the Oddaverjar's interest in sponsoring Thorlák was genuine. The priests in that family were good men with good intentions, and their support of the Church was sincere. However, their political aspirations often colored their interpretations of what good intentions were. It was just as advantageous as it was generous to offer Thorlák the opportunity to study in continental Europe. He would excel there just as he had at Oddi, but now under the auspices of better known and more influential players in the Catholic Church. The Abbey School of St. Victor in Paris was gaining a reputation among the Scandinavian elite as a worthy place of study. Likewise, England offered several renowned centers for theological study. Under the mentorship of French or English clerics, Thorlák could advance quickly and, with his mother and sisters still living in Iceland; he surely would apportion his favor and fortune accordingly. He would make a fine emissary between his Oddaverjar foster-family and the political movers in whatever country he visited.

By the time the Oddaverjar came with their offer, Thorlák had acquired a small amount of assets for himself which he applied toward his travel expenses. He met the prospect with both eagerness and trepidation. He felt a certain reluctance to spend his assets on travel while leaving his family behind to be provided for by others in his absence. Yet, he felt a deep obligation of gratitude to his mentors, and would never be so inhospitable as to refuse such a magnanimous gesture. If they saw fit to send him to the continent to study, then it was his duty to rise to the task and do well by Father Eyjólfur, who was as much a father to him as a teacher.

Finally, it was agreed: Thorlák would commence studies at the Augustinian Abbey School of St. Victor in Paris, France. This was the school made famous by Hugh of St. Victor, whose writings on the Sacraments were legendary; a place where virtue was considered on even par with knowledge; and a frequent destination of the likes of Bernard of Clairvaux and Thomas Becket.

Thorlák's voyage from Iceland to the European Continent would take at least eight days under the most favorable conditions. The Faroe, Orkney and Shetland islands are the first land to greet him after the long initial span of North Atlantic is crossed, but then the expanse along the length of England relies on favorable winds to make in less than a full week.

Journeys at sea had always called to Thorlák's imagination. Experiencing this in all five senses was exhilarating. While many of his shipmates grumbled at being confined at sea, Thorlák observed everything with interest and felt a close connection to his seafaring ancestors. He wondered if his own father felt mesmerized by the sheer breadth of the sky, the tease of the elusive horizon and the seeming infinity of the stars.

He grieved that he never knew these aspects of his father. He may have had the good sense and practical instincts of his mother, but Thorlák's love of contemplation and deep spiritual musing were not qualities she shared. In fact, she seemed quick to dismiss these aspects of Thorlák's personality as shyness and reticence, not understanding how he lost himself chasing thoughts and loved every moment of the chase. Halla pointedly quipped from time to time that her husband had all the qualities of a successful man but wasted opportunity by dawdling on pointless ideas rather than finishing tasks at hand.

Thorlák felt obligated not to make these mistakes himself; yet he had learned over the years to indulge in this forbidden pleasure of wasting time when nobody else was around. He often did this at night, turning restless sleep into long, luxurious stretches of uninhibited contemplation on anything that happened to enter his mind. Summer nights as mid-dawn afforded him a second day to crown the first eighteen hours of earnest labor. Winter nights, on the other hand, yielded an audience with the stars between heavenly displays of aurora lights.

Here, at sea, the physical waters swept Thorlák along in the same manner as his inner thoughts. He felt a great release as he realized his wishes of being carried off to faraway lands on the wings of the wind. He contributed his share of labor to his shipmates by day, but by night, he gave himself over to the invisible air currents lifting the sails… moving the waves… caressing his face… keeping time with the rhythm of his breathing.

After spending more than a week in surreality, the ship reached the Suðursjór, the South Sea, and the harbors of France. As he disembarked, Thorlák both felt the ground beneath his feet, and the terror of being completely alone in a foreign land.

CHAPTER SIX

PARIS THEN LINCOLN

Thorlák had some idea of what to expect in Paris from what he had studied in Iceland, but the reality of the actual city before him was overwhelming. Never before had he beheld this vast a testimony to man's capacity for building. Iceland's landscape was itself a towering stone majesty, to be sure, but here, the stone was hewn and shaped and laid to make roads and ramparts and imposing structures. Architecture he once only imagined was suddenly alive and soaring before him in aesthetic wonder. Surrounding him were merchants showcasing an unfathomable wealth of goods, many of which he could not recognize. The constant motion of people from every social class reminded him how royalty was present and revered in this land… and that, as a priest, his was a place among the nobility. He could not comprehend how he was any more important than anyone here, especially being the son of a seafarer-merchant father and a mother living as a house servant on a chieftain's estate. His humility instilled in him a deep sense of obligation to live up to his vows to his people, and to Almighty God.

Thorlák's overpowering awe of the European continent was a veiled blessing. He felt more vulnerable here than even as the bewildered nine year old expected to assume the duties of his absent father. Yet as this child he had been so earnestly inquisitive and compliant that he developed an instinctive trust in the mentorship of his elders. Now, at the age of twenty, the priests and brothers accepting him under their tutelage would fit that role for him once again.

Being the protégé of the scholarly Oddaverjar clan ensured that Thorlák would be well provided for both in his personal needs and in his education. The Augustinian monks at the Abbey of St. Victor, located near the left bank of the Seine River, warmly received Thorlák among the other scholars in residence from all parts of Europe. All trepidation quickly faded from Thorlák's mind as he realized he had found a glorious sanctuary of like minds, letters, discipline, and prayer.

The Victorine Augustinians were a thriving Parisian monastic community founded in 1108 by William of Champeaux, Archdeacon and philosopher, who was himself seeking to retire to a simpler lifestyle rooted in prayer and theological study. He had been a close associate of Bernard of Clairvaux, the saintly scholar and founder of the Cistercian Order, and was heavily influenced by his teachings. Yet William was equally attracted to the Rule of St. Augustine and the discipline of the Augustinian Canons Regular. He began observing the Augustinian rule and decided to form a community at the shrine of St. Victor, to which he would retreat into retirement. The community soon attracted many of William's associates and former students who persuaded him out of retirement to form a school at the shrine sponsored by many patrons from among the academic and clerical elite. From there the Abbey of St. Victor was established as a monastery by its own right and a school for both the monks in residence and many visiting scholars who came from far and wide to observe this greatly celebrated gathering of academics, mystics, and ascetics.

Thorlák entered the school during the height of the influence of Hugh of St. Victor, whose rich legacy of theological methodology demonstrated how academic study can, and should, lead one to a deeper understanding and experience of God. In his simple and earnest way, Thorlák already lived out this ideal. He ordinarily went about his days pondering the wonder of God and Creation, and every bit of knowledge he acquired since childhood felt to him a joy. Learning was a treat, not a chore, when each new concept permitted him that much more clarity on God's workings. He was a natural fit with the Augustinian philosophy taught by the Canons at St. Victor.

Among the Victorine courses were studies on the sacraments, preaching, sacred liturgy and administration of parishes. Overarching all was the imperative that, in each aspect of his priesthood, every man must first aspire toward virtue. According to the Victorines, love of God and excellence in the spiritual life must drive all other pursuits. This not only held fast to the rigorous tenets of St. Augustine, but it also reflected the spirit of reform spreading throughout the Catholic Church in Europe. Since the later years of the eleventh century, the decrees of Pope Gregory VII called the entire hierarchy of the Catholic Church worldwide to account for its motives, its morality and its embodiment of the Kingdom of God on earth. Pope Gregory took this term literally, seeking to define the Catholic Church as a sovereign body with a moral law encompassing all other bodies of governance. He felt the Church should be unified and centralized. He supported the idea church property should be held by the central ecclesial body, not by individuals or families, which echoed his condemnation of simony and other abuses of the priestly class for personal gain. Pope Gregory also wanted priests to live by the highest moral standards across the board. Furthermore, he asserted that men pursuing the priesthood should not be married or seek to cultivate marriage. Priestly celibacy was a discipline, a sacrifice and a demonstration of allegiance to serving God's church, the Bride referenced in Sacred Scripture and in St. Augustine's writings on the psalms and Old Testament prophecy.

Icelanders knew very little of these reforms, being over a thousand miles removed from mainland Europe and putting higher priority on mere survival than acquiring virtue in the harsh conditions of the far north. There were few pleasures to be had outside of satisfying the drives of human nature. It not only seemed ludicrous to consider ascetic sacrifice, it was categorically dismissed by most of the clergy who reasoned that these ideas simply did not apply to those outside of the immediate circles of those people proposing them.

As his schooling went on, Thorlák had no doubt in his mind that this was the life he had been drawn toward since his earliest awareness. These were not radically challenging ideas to him; they were affirmations of truths he had known deep in his heart, but only now heard articulated in ways that were practical – and, for the first time, seemed attainable. Day after day he lived in the harmony of the Augustinian Canons and witnessed the Gospels in action and imagined how easily this pattern of living could be applied among the clergy in Iceland. It would take persuading, at first, and would require a certain period of instruction. But, if enough men gave this way of life a try, they would soon see that the discipline required was much more a matter of shaping habits than anything that would cause suffering. His mentors among the Oddaverjar would surely welcome his rapidly forming plans for a stronger priesthood and more dignified morality for all of Iceland.

Thorlák made the most of every moment in this academic oasis. He did not much avail himself of the city itself. Any of his cosmopolitan curiosity was satisfied, good measure and flowing over, within the abundant endowment of the Victorine library; besides, the unending sightline of walls and streets and busy people made him uneasily aware of how far he was from home. His reclusiveness attracted many comments about Iceland's backwardness and the gratitude he must feel toward the opportunity to better himself here. The general sense of the Parisians was that Icelanders were crude and ruthless Viking scavengers – which left him deeply wounded. He was well aware of Iceland's history and how it must seem to others, yet he knew the farmers and merchants and fishermen back home were resourceful, dedicated and kind-hearted people. It troubled him that even the priests and brothers in the God-filled halls of the abbey could so easily forget the sacred spark of humanity dwelling in those outside their own circles. Once more, Thorlák kept many of his thoughts to himself, absorbing his free time with books more than idle conversation.

As he always had, Thorlák rapidly absorbed all he could through reading and observation. By the time his studies were complete, Thorlák was amply equipped to bring these precepts of theological formation and ecclesial reform anywhere he might go forth. By comparable note, other associates of the School of St. Victor at that time were the soon-to-be Archbishop of Canterbury, Thomas Becket, and future Norwegian Archbishop of Nidaros, Eysteinn Erlendsson. The latter would prove to be a providential connection, as both the Skálholt and Hólar dioceses of Iceland answered to the See of the Archdiocese of Nidaros, and it was advantageous to have this common frame of reference. These men, however, were far more accomplished, and considerably older, than their Icelandic contemporary in his twenties who had so far only had a few years' experience in very small parishes. What Thorlák lacked in experience, they soon saw, he made up for in scholastic achievement. The suggestion was made toward the end of his stay that a man of his aptitude would do very well to make himself proficient in the *Decretum Gratiani* – the newly codified canon law. With such mastery, Thorlák's career could reach the highest of offices, if he so chose. According to Thomas Becket and his legal-minded contemporaries, the place to do this was undoubtedly the Cathedral School of Lincoln, England, which was well-populated by juridical priest scholars with high ambitions. Thomas ought to know; he himself had been a protégé of Lincoln's Bishop, Robert de Chesney, who oversaw the Cathedral School. Thorlák's teachers agreed, and so did his sponsors back home, the Oddaverjar. Arrangements were made to extend Thorlák's education between connections in Paris, Iceland and England with valuable goods exchanged in the process. Iceland could not routinely offer much in the way of trade with the exception of things difficult to find elsewhere, such as narwhal tusks, which were found only in the Arctic seas and prized by mainland Europeans.

Always amazed by the privileges offered him, Thorlák accepted with wonder and humble gratitude. He did not consider himself ambitious in his career, but he was diligent and prudent in everything he undertook. He felt it would be of great profit to be able to return to Iceland and perhaps be the first to formally instruct the clerics there about this recently decreed universal law of the church. His mentors had no idea of the small but sincere scope of Thorlák's aspirations. They imagined no less for him than a diocese of his own, with connections throughout the European continent and a keen memory for those who brought him there. How each side's prayers would be heard and answered would be seen only through the Providence of God Himself.

Thorlák had never much felt at home in Paris, yet he found it difficult to gather his belongings for the voyage to England. He knew instinctively that he would not likely return. As confining as he felt his surroundings to be, he savored the Abbey's rhythm of hymn, prayer, and study. It felt as natural as breathing to align one's self so closely with God's order and he had no idea what would await him outside these man-made stone walls. This sailing would be a much shorter journey with barely any chance to retreat to his thoughts. Within two days he was standing on new ground.

If the first sight of Paris had overwhelmed Thorlák's senses, the vista of Lincoln before him now staggered his mind on a scale he could not describe. In one glance was both the enormous Norman castle of William the Conqueror and the massive Cathedral of the Blessed Virgin Mary. Thorlák stood and stared. He had seen majestic heights at home. The Seljalandsfoss waterfall was nearly two hundred feet tall when viewed from the lowland below and yet the Cathedral rose even higher in its heavenward reach. He had never before felt insignificant when facing such great height, but here he became acutely aware of his smallness, and it was not the kind of awe he was used to. Thorlák recalled the words of King Solomon: "I have indeed built a magnificent temple for you, O God; a place for you to dwell forever." Even so, Thorlák could not have imagined the grandeur of this Cathedral if he had not seen it before him.

The Cathedral School at Lincoln was a different place from St. Victor altogether, given that it was not its own abbey but part of the enormous household of the Bishop of the largest geographical diocese in England. Still, the Augustinian Canons were well represented throughout Lincolnshire and their influence was widespread. The school itself was just as rigorous and well-endowed academically as the School of St. Victor, and Thorlák was impressed to be surrounded by such urbane and knowledgeable scholars.

Canon Law was in its earliest development when Thorlák came to Lincoln. The Decretum Gratiani was the first time the entire body of laws of the

Catholic Church had been gathered into one cohesive work. Compiled by Gratian, a monk in Northern Italy, the Decretum was a curation and examination of every known statute of the Catholic Church from the apostles onward. For each discrepancy and contradiction, Gratian gave a dialectical commentary attempting to tease out the law's actual intent and application. It was a comprehensive work that sought to codify and standardize Church law throughout the world, and Thorlák found it an invaluable study. Here was a resource that would build the faith of the Church from the top down in its administration and the bottom up in its application. It outlined a standard morality for priests and aspirations toward holiness for the laity. Gratian's rationale was immediately apparent to him and the dialectical approach appealed greatly to Thorlák's mind. He learned how to see both the reality before him and the ideal to which laws were directed… and then, the conceptual path to synthesize the two, as though a map from what is now to what is meant to be.

With the discipline and virtuous aspiration of the Augustinian Canons, and the textual knowledge of the Decretum Gratiani, Father Thorlák

Thórhallsson completed his studies in 1159. Equipped as he was for an illustrious career ahead, he took his belongings and provisions and set out to fulfill his destiny – just as he had planned. He sailed from England, with great resolve, to resume his priesthood in Iceland.

CHAPTER SEVEN

RETURN TO ICELAND

At the age of twenty six, Thorlák could say he was an ordained priest, a world traveler, an accomplished theologian and a scholar of Canon Law. From these connections, his name was now known among the Church hierarchy in England, France and Norway. Everyone he encountered, from those heading the important institutions to the servants of the households in which he stayed, remembered him not for being the young man from faraway Iceland, but because he was so genial and good-natured, and such an excellent listener. He had a way of making each person feel like it was his privilege to be greeted by them – and, although they could not have known this, it was an absolutely genuine sentiment on his part. Thorlák never lost his sense of marvel and gratitude that he, such an ordinary person from a laborer's land, could have opportunities bringing him to such high social circles. He had truly risen above the lot of most Icelanders, and he exalted this only in so far as it reflected that one aspect of his identity: an Icelander.

He could barely contain his jubilation at seeing the volcanic mountains in the far distance as his ship concluded the final and longest leg of the journey home across the North Sea. He ached for the familiarity of home, and if the ship's men had not needed to secure their vessel on shore, he would surely have been the first off, laden as he was with his belongings and gifts he had brought for his family and benefactors.

The hailing of his friends and relatives reached him before he had the opportunity to speak. His mother was overjoyed at his sight, and her embrace was a tender sweetness he savored for having gone six years without the affections of family to succor his spirits. One after another, kinsfolk and well-wishers, parishioners and friends of friends feted his return in grand succession. Between breaths he caught sight of his sister Ragnheið and turned to greet her… and noticed she held the hand of a small boy, possibly three or four years old. He looked at once at her and the child, seeing the unmistakable resemblance of their eyes, and he stooped down to take a closer look. Standing tall again, he looked inquisitively at Ragnheið, who proudly said, "This is Páll – your nephew! My son!"

The others' voices faded into the background as Thorlák gazed in surprise and delight at the child before him. Ragnheið spoke again. "Páll! This is your uncle, Thorlák. He is my brother!" She lifted Páll on to her hip so he could take a closer look. The boy studied the face of this man who was completely unfamiliar to him yet smiled warmly. Thorlák looked back at Ragnheið, who said, softly, "Páll is the son of Jón."

Thorlák's eyes widened as he considered what this meant, and still he said nothing. He glanced around. Jón Loftsson was somewhere in this crowd, most likely with the Oddaverjar clansmen who were together in their own contingency with the priests and deacons of the nearby districts. Bishop Klæng, who had been appointed the year before Thorlák left, and Gizur Hallsson, who had almost held that office himself, were both in attendance among the priests, the teachers from the School at Oddi, and several Þingmenn, the members of the national assembly, who gathered together for this homecoming celebration.

He touched Páll softly on the head, moving his lips in a silent prayer of blessing and concluding by tracing the sign of the cross with his thumb: first on the boy's forehead, then his lips, then his chest. He looked intently into Páll's eyes and paused a moment before saying, loudly enough this time to be heard, "With the Lord's guidance, may this child restore honor to our family and glory to God through whichever office to which he is called." Ragnheið was deeply touched by this blessing, but before she could speak, Thorlák turned to her and said, quietly, "As for you, may you repent of the grave dishonor brought upon our family to have allowed your affections to cultivate iniquity in the heart of a married man."

The shock of this admonishment so closely following his heartfelt blessing infuriated Ragnheið. Upon catching her breath, she snapped in reply, "If there is iniquity being cultivated, it is in the farce that an imposed marriage contract is morally superior to the genuine love between a man and a woman!" Building momentum, she continued: "This child is the great-grandson of a king! He brings more honor to our family than anything you might learn in just six years… and, for all this celebration of your achievement, it seems you have not learned anything of much real use!"

Halla, Thorlák's mother, quickly interjected. "This is not the time for this sort of debate. Thorlák is merely surprised, as we should have expected him to be, but he is not so foolish as to dismiss the son of royal blood – or the son of one of his benefactors. He has always been a little slower to consider such things, but he will see that you have done very well by our family – in ways your father never could."

The rapid unfolding of all these realizations at once was overwhelming. Thorlák felt stunned. Within a short span he had gone from the safe enclosure of academia to the surging anticipation of seeing his homeland once again – to this jagged image of just how far his world at home was removed from the sanctuaries of virtue from which he returned.

CHAPTER EIGHT

THORLAK THE FOOL

It took several weeks for Thorlák to become acclimated once more to the priest's life in Iceland. He took turns staying in the households of extended family members and various members of his foster-family, the Oddaverjar. Along the way, he assisted at each respective farmstead church and developed for himself a routine which hearkened closely to the Augustinian Canons' daily structure. He found it very well to awaken early and begin his day in prayer, singing the morning-songs from both hymnal and Psalter as the Canons had done each day at dawn. In this way, he found his day imbued with a deep connection to God in Heaven in all that he did. It also connected him in mind to the Church, the Body of Christ, present in each place yet also in every other locale throughout the world. Before traveling to the continent, he had not given much thought to locations outside of Iceland. Now he could imagine the true immensity of many other lands and seas and people at once… and realized the true scope of Catholic Church *on earth*.

Thorlák was very content in his state in life. He served God, and the people he loved, and prayed for everyone with deeper reverence each passing day. He made sure that his mother and sisters had all they needed materially and spiritually. Halla remained well on the estate at Oddi. With Eyvǫr, she gave much help to Ragnheið, who not only had Páll, but had begun showing signs that another child was on the way. It was confirmed in 1160 when she gave birth to her second son, Örm; and as before, there was no question as to who the baby's father was. By this time, Jón was fully occupied with his political career, well on his way to becoming one of Iceland's most powerful chieftains. He also acquired three other concubines besides Ragnheið – and, of course, kept his wife, Halldora, at home. Between wife and four mistresses, Jón was father to nine children. As was still the case, Jón's prominence gave great leeway to his behavior. The women bearing his children felt privileged, not scandalized, and Jón himself was quite proud of his progeny.

Thorlák was greatly troubled by Jón's cavalier disregard for moral law. The priest-teachers at Oddi, starting with Sæmundur Froði, formed their students in the same Catholic faith as the virtuous students under Hugh of St. Victor, who himself traced his teaching all the way back to St. Augustine, and ultimately, Jesus Christ Himself. St. Augustine, in his pivotal *City of God*, was clear about moral certitude and the persistence of right even when it was contradicted by public opinion. Jón was not exempt from moral accountability no matter how much support he had from the *goðar*.

Icelanders considered themselves unique among world governments for cultivating a parliamentary system rather than a monarchy, and for this they took great pride as a people. The *Þingmenn* and *goðar* governed by popular consensus. When laws no longer made sense, they changed them. By the same token, if other countries' laws did not make sense, Icelanders felt no need to abide by them.

The laws of the Church seemed like a fair subset of rules, even if they were imposed from outside of Iceland. "Thou Shalt Not Kill" and "Thou Shalt Not Steal" were sensible and essential statutes of civilized conduct. "Thou Shalt Not Commit Adultery" was a little more ambiguous, especially when marriage was a contractual alliance between families for the primary purpose of growing and maintaining property holdings. Life expectancy was not good, and infant mortality was high. Did it matter all that greatly if children were borne by wife or by concubine, so long as they lived past infancy and were provided for fairly by their father? In contractual terms, modifications to sacramental marriage made sense… and, common sense was the prevailing standard over moral conduct.

Clergy, too, had a favorably sustainable system that made better sense in terms of civil law than Canon Law. Priests who married could guarantee property on which churches could be built and maintained. Priests with sons could keep the priestly line going through many generations, and with food in constantly short supply, it was advantageous to band together in marital unity than to try and subsist on one's own. Single, celibate priesthood just did not make sense in Icelandic society. As with every other instance of law, if priests could not see a sufficiently obvious reason to remain single, the notion was disregarded without much fear or repercussion.

Thorlák saw in stark truth that his education did much more than advance his development or his career. It revealed, painfully, the absence of virtue among his mentors and kinsfolk. His fluency in Canon Law made it clear just how far astray the Church in Iceland had drifted from the ordinary conduct and laws of the Catholic Church. He spent many hours pondering all of this as he went about the countryside, praying for guidance as the discrepancy gnawed at his heart. How could he have been given such a rich education only to be asked to turn a blind eye to the deterioration of his mentors – who not only abused the offices of the Catholic Church, but flagrantly encouraged others to do so? He knew he had every capability of pursuing a satisfying career among like-minded people back on the continent, but he could not reconcile the idea of leaving Iceland in its state of moral decay. He could not participate in such hypocrisy without bringing great disgrace to his teachers and the principles they imparted. All of this seemed to him a call, an obligation before all else, to set things right as a representative of God and His Church.

He prayed day and night about this dilemma. His mentors and kinsfolk carried on as they were accustomed, oblivious of any impropriety in their conduct.

Familiar as they were with the reputation of St. Victor's, Thorlák's benefactors still found it puzzling that he would take the intangible aspects of his education, such as striving toward virtue, as seriously as the practical information he acquired. Surely he would not expect Icelanders to conform to the conventions put forth in a Parisian setting – or, was this a case of Thorlák taking matters too literally? One of the faults often found with Thorlák in his student days was his difficulty grasping figurative speech. He tended to see things at face value, struggling to pick up on nuances. It was not a prohibitive matter as a student, but as a priest, Thorlák was criticized more than once for the rigidity of his interpretations of Scripture and church rubrics. As people became vexed by his analysis, he justified his positions using dialectics to show the kernels of truth on both sides of the matter. In most cases, he acceded to his critics, preferring peaceful disagreement to contentious argument.

As time went on, Thorlák's patrons among the Oddaverjar grew increasingly restless with his contentment as a district priest. They did not want his education wasted on the common folk of the

Icelandic countryside. Thorlák showed no interest in further travel, claiming he could not stray far from his mother or sisters, whose care he took all the more seriously as he observed men of marrying age tending the needs of their families at great labor and expense. Thorlák's kinfolk and mentors all felt he belonged in higher standing and blamed his youth for his naïveté. If he was determined to stay in Iceland, his mentors considered how he could build more of a domestic career.

He could begin acquiring property of his own. With his management skills, he could easily gain clout as a householder, perhaps overseeing multiple churches or constructing a large church complex on his estate. Many possibilities existed in this arena, and if Thorlák was more of a practical man, this might be best use of his skill.

Thorlák had not been home long enough to have acquired much since his return. His kinsfolk had a lucrative solution: Thorlák could propose marriage to a widow with substantial property. Such arrangements were common among the clergy. A widow was free to marry and already had a good amount of property. A priest could bring in revenue by using her property for church purposes, guaranteeing safety and prosperity for a woman who otherwise fending for herself. Thorlák's elders approached him assertively with this idea, and were just as assertively opposed.

Thorlák quoted Canon Law, stating a priest was to remain single and celibate as the Bridegroom solely of Holy Church. Marriage, even to a worthy widow, was contrary to the singular call of a priest to his vocation. His mentors argued with him, citing copious examples of married priests who lived holy lives and provided well for the women they took as their own. Here again, the gray areas of reasoning did not persuade their literal-minded protégé. Thorlák meticulously explained in dialectical fashion how nothing is lost by betrothing one's self to a holy vocation. Furthermore, as representatives of Jesus Christ, priests are called to live in ways that set higher standards than ordinary men, so that ordinary men in turn can reach higher toward holiness. He acknowledged their reasoning within their interpretation of right and wrong, but ultimately, he came back to Canon Law and asserted his allegiance with gentle but firm insistence.

The Oddaverjar were not satisfied.

A small contingency of Thorlák's relatives confronted him, saying that his desire to live a holy life, while noble in theory, was not realistic. How ludicrous, they said, to think that the Catholic Church could be codified into a single set of laws that applied the same way in every different country! He was too young to know how ridiculous he sounded, and so, for his own good, they told him straight out that his refusal to go along with this idea made him look like a fool.

Besides, they said, what would become of his mother, and his sisters? Would they remain servants of the Oddaverjar for the rest of their lives? Or would Thorlák finally provide them with a real home – as a real family, of good name once more?

Thorlák was greatly discouraged. Men he looked up to, and trusted... his relatives, his benefactors, his mentors... were all saying he was in error. He began to doubt his judgment. What if he really was naïve? He always had a peculiar wisdom in the way he considered things, and up until now, people praised him for it. He was compliant, agreeable, well-liked by his elders... and now, for the first time, he had failed to win their approval.

Uncertainty filled his mind as he tried within himself to find the truth dialectically.

The beleaguered priest took his interior conflict out into the quiet solitude of the night, peering at the stars and begging in prayer for direction. His mind was very clear on what was right. He only wavered because the people he trusted were so adamant that he was making a huge mistake. They seemed not to know him at all. But if he ignored their guidance, and they were correct, what would this mean for his integrity as a priest – or as a person?

He wished for a fleeting moment that his father were there to advise him. His father, whom his family also called foolish on many occasions, might not have the right answer, but he would surely understand how Thorlák felt.

In the endless night before him, he found no sympathy, and no direction for how to proceed. He let his own thoughts unspool and was reminded of another night, not unlike this one, when he felt like he did not know himself. He replayed the same questions he had that night, with the same temptation tormenting his heart and mind. How did he know, for certain, that he was actually meant to live a priestly life? What if this was the chance he had been promised, to fulfill his ache to be a father and householder and provider to his own family?

It felt horribly wrong when he imagined taking over the property of a woman who had lost her husband, and taking the place that had been vacated by the death of her spouse.

He imagined this widow as a person. Was she younger? Older? A mother? Childless? Would he be her stability, her reassurance, in a sweeping act of charity? Was this what Psalm 146 meant, that the Lord looks after the widow and the orphan?

Thorlák grew restless... then, angry. The longer he prayed, the angrier he felt: at his mentors, for confusing him, and at his inability to answer their arguments. He vividly recalled his mystical experience of the Blessed Virgin Mary and wondered if it all came down to this defining moment, where he wanted only to obey what was right but felt like his interior compass was spinning between false norths.

Into the night, Thorlák exclaimed, *"I DO NOT KNOW WHAT WILL HAPPEN!"*

He stood, in the response of silence, and concluded that he would leave this decision in the hands of Mary herself. If this were part of the design she promised, then he would not stand in her way. But, neither would he eagerly run toward something that felt wrong on every level.

CHAPTER NINE

THE WIDOW

Thorlák's relatives had already begun making inquiries on his behalf of the eligible widows in the south of Iceland. He met their request with resignation, telling them that he would consider their proposition and proceed as the matter transpired.

It happened that there was a widow with a farmstead at Háf, situated near the Þjorsá River north of the Hekla volcano – not far from Oddi, and in the region dominated by the Oddaverjar. Thorlák's relatives believed her to be a suitable and strategic political match, particularly as her estate included a church building. Initial inquiries found her amenable to the idea. More importantly, she herself had ties to one of the other influential families in the diocese. Hoping to beat Thorlák at his own game, his mentors approached him with the idea that marrying this widow would not only yield a prosperous church-farmstead, but politically would allow him to more easily advance his agenda for shaping the priesthood in Skálholt. They asserted that, if reform was something Thorlák wanted to pursue, this would give him an opening and a platform.

He was not impressed with their logic but kept his thoughts silent. He agreed to meet the widow at a reception given for both families on her farmstead. His relatives were delighted, and the parties convened in a festive gathering soon thereafter.

When Thorlák was formally introduced to the widow, she graciously greeted him with a firm handshake and a confident smile. He liked her. She was attractive to him both in appearance and intelligence. Her face was fair, and her tightly fastened hair was likely long and flowing when released. The Rule of Saint Augustine forbade men from gazing upon women because the beauty of the opposite sex was a reality that men could not possibly deny, and which could quickly become alluring when pondered for more than a moment. He let his eyes linger a bit longer before looking away. He seldom permitted himself the indulgence of looking upon a woman in the way a man might approach his wife. He waited, cautiously, for the thrill of the moment – but found instead a sincere admiration for this woman before him. He saw her strength, and resourcefulness, and the intelligence in her smile… and, thus, her worth. She was worthy by her own accord, not based on any of the property to which she was entitled by family or marriage. She was indeed a worthy woman.

He turned his gaze to others in the room, feeling a sense of optimism building in his mind. Somehow, he knew things were to be exactly as they should be, and that this episode would prove pivotal in his life as a priest. He had no idea how this might be, but a feeling of confidence would not leave him.

The dinner proceeded well into the night, and the guests at last began to retreat. Those in Thorlák's party were shown to the guest-house and bade góða nótt by their hosts. His relatives were pleased with how well things were progressing. Without question, a marriage proposition would be drawn up soon, and the matter would be settled at last.

As always, Thorlák found it difficult to fall asleep. His kinsfolk were soundly slumbering well before he became drowsy, and his thoughts were plentiful in the dark. He prayed, continuously, that God's will be accomplished through this episode at hand, and that he be shown the path to obedience. In the silence he recalled Psalm 119:

Blessed are those whose ways are blameless,
who walk according to the law of the LORD.
Blessed are those who keep his statutes
and seek him with all their heart—
they do no wrong
but follow his ways.
You have laid down precepts
that are to be fully obeyed.
Oh, that my ways were steadfast
in obeying your decrees!
Then I would not be put to shame
when I consider all your commands.
I will praise you with an upright heart
as I learn your righteous laws.
I will obey your decrees;
do not utterly forsake me.

At those last words, he felt again the reassurance that his yearning for obedience would not go unheard. He began to drift into sleep… but sat up, alert, at the countenance of a man standing at the foot of his bed.

He was dumbfounded. He heard nobody enter, and the room was completely dim. How is it that this man was before him, fully visible? As he focused in the dark, he could easily see this was not one of his relatives, nor one of the widow's relatives. This was – a prince? Someone of nobility, based on the splendor of their attire. He could barely comprehend what was before him.

The man addressed him. "What would your mission be here, if you could decide?"

Thorlák answered, stupefied, in the words he had uttered the previous night: "I do not know what will happen."

The man continued. "I know that you intend to ask for a wife here. But you must not let that matter come up, because that will not happen. A much better bride is intended for you, and you shall take no other."

At that, the man vanished completely from sight.

Thorlák bolted from his bed and out the guest house door. There was no trace of any visitor departing from any direction. He was incredulous and nearly giddy as he began to realize his prayer had been heard, and answered most definitively. If only – if only his relatives had witnessed this magnificent apparition!

He was alone, again, in the darkness, but filled with laughter and wonder. He had no doubt been visited by a heavenly messenger with clear direction and vindication of his adherence to the way of virtue. He burst out words of praise to Almátturgur Guð and in his elation inadvertently roused the widow, who met him outside the main door of the house.

"Í nafni Almáttugs Guðs!" – That is, in the name of Almighty God – "what is the matter with you?!"

The animated cleric rushed to greet his hostess, taking her by both hands and exclaiming, "IN THE NAME OF ALMIGHTY GOD, ICELAND HAS BEEN FAVORED BY THE LORD!"

Before she could express her puzzlement, Thorlák uncharacteristically began speaking, excitedly and fluently in his exuberance. He explained everything – his dilemma, his relatives' insistence, his belief in a higher order of morality for the priesthood, and his wish that the clerical standards of Canon Law might become the norm throughout Iceland. He gushed with enthusiasm such that she had no opportunity to interrupt or question him – and his zeal was so pure, so passionate, that she had no desire for him to stop. He had at once a child's wonder and a sage's wisdom. Never before had she seen anyone speak with such fervor, and she was completely captivated. She might have given him half her property if he had asked, but instead, he begged her understanding about rescinding the proposition of marriage, repeating several times that it had no bearing on her worthiness whatsoever. She assured him, yes, this seemed very reasonable – in fact, noble of him – to uphold his office of the priesthood in such reverence. She herself was a devout woman and was touched by the keenness of his faith. She promised most sincerely to lend her support in any way she could be helpful to him in his priestly efforts. She further pledged her family's backing for whatever he had in mind that inspired him to such a degree that he might proclaim the greatness of God in the middle of the night.

Catching his breath, he thanked the widow profusely, and paused to gaze fully into her bright blue eyes. She was indeed a special woman, who could so quickly forgive one who reneged on his marital contract before it was even ratified. He thanked God for her, aloud, and commanded that she get back to sleep. Smiling, she complied, returning inside. Thorlák remained outdoors, whispering prayers and hymns of praise until the morning light dawned.

As day broke, the men in Thorlák's party began preparing for the important matters ahead. They noticed their protégé had already risen. On searching for him, he greeted them at the door with as much enthusiasm as he had shown the unsuspecting widow – except, his relatives were not as charmed. They protested, loudly, that his behavior was outlandish. Some questioned if he had spent the night drinking ale, but others who knew him well reminded them that he had a strong aversion to any spirited beverage. They passed his chatter off as nervous prattle and proceeded to the main house of the farmstead. There, to their astonishment, the widow's kinfolk greeted them with the same news: there would be no proposition of marriage. Quarreling broke out among everyone there. The widow herself attempted to maintain order, shouting over the din that this had been a mutually favorable decision. At last she appealed to her farmhands to disperse the crowd, and the parties drew back into their own circles. Thorlák took the hands of his hostess one last time and gave her a particular blessing which she received with great satisfaction before bidding him farewell. He returned to the group with his kinsfolk and set off for the journey home.

As anticipated, Thorlák endured a barrage of criticism and questions from every direction. He walked on, silent, for several hundred yards, and then turned to face his fellow travelers.

He spoke: "My good men: I am sure you are wondering at the abruptness with which my determination appears to have changed. I assure you, what you have witnessed is nothing less than the work of Almighty God, and a marvelous portent of great things for Iceland!"

He proceeded to explain the entire story of the angelic appearance and the widow's assent. He spoke with such conviction that nobody doubted he was telling the truth. Astonished, they listened, attentively, and concluded that his decision was inescapable. Reluctant as they were to admit, it did seem, for lack of any other explanation, that Almighty God looked favorably on raising the virtue of the clergy in Iceland… and, that Thorlák had been the first to notice.

CHAPTER TEN

KIRKJUBÆR

In the year 1162, Thorlák became acquainted with a householder-priest in the southeast named Bjarnheðinn ("Bjarni") Sigurðarson. Bjarni took an immediate liking to this young, affable priest, and they soon discovered they had similar dispositions both in their approach to the priesthood and life in general. Their conversations brought them great satisfaction and inspiration. Thorlák, of course, had extensively more education and academic knowledge than Bjarni; but Bjarni had grown up in a large, loving family and had what Thorlák felt was an innate expertise in the science and essence of human relationships. The two would easily talk for great lengths about human nature, the longings of the human heart, and the revelations of God's love through the very existence of Jesus as Man and Redeemer.

After many such conversations, Bjarni invited his friend to take up residence with him, in his household at Kirkjubær in the region of Siða. Together, they would serve as parish priests, supporting one another in both ministry and

household.   Thorlák eagerly agreed, and with great
joy he called this his new home. He suggested that
he and Bjarni order their days around a regular
routine. They would rise early each morning to
pray the office of readings together; then, read and
reflect on the day's Scripture; then, pray specifically
for people in their parish; and then, at last, go about
their work – be this priestly duties or the upkeep of
the farmstead. The men found they were especially
drawn to the Gospel passage of Matthew 18:20,
*"Where two or more are gathered in My Name, I AM with
them."* The priests adopted this as a pastoral maxim
for themselves, and everyone in their parish would
surely agree that they carried an essence of holiness
about them, as though Christ Himself was close at
hand wherever they went. Many said the household
at Kirkjubær felt like a monastery in their midst,
such was the harmony and grace that flowed from
the two priests living and working there. Thorlák
felt great satisfaction. Surely, this was his heart's
yearning fulfilled: he was the provider for a church,
a farmstead, and a throng of people he considered a
spiritual family. The countryside at Siða was equally
delightful to the eyes and heart, with vast green
stretches of grass and moss guarded by great
columns of basalt cliffs, from which cascade the

stunning vertical drop of the *Foss á Síðu.* The *Dverghamrar* rock formations flanking the base of the waterfall made the entire area a contrast of rolling bright valley and imposing dark monolith.

In the years they worked together, Séra Thorlák and Séra Bjarni served that region excellently.

Their priestly conversations continued all the more as they resided together. In Paris, Thorlák had been immersed in the teachings of Hugh of St. Victor, which he now imparted to Bjarni in his own words. Victorine themes often centered on love – the incomprehensible *agape* God has for us, and the restless longing of the human heart for God. Hugh of St. Victor himself had drawn great inspiration from St. Augustine in his writings, and he gave an astute treatment on *caritas* within the rich context of Augustinian theology. Bjarni found it amazing that Thorlák could explain such complex teachings in ways that were immediately meaningful and practical – yet, Thorlák relied just as greatly on Bjarni to know if his application of all he had learned was relevant, or realistic. After all, they were called to serve their fellow Icelanders – not a cosmopolitan city like Paris.

Still, Thorlák had a sense that the spiritual life of Iceland was not likely to progress toward holiness under the leadership there. He mused that there would be a much better chance of raising Iceland to holiness by inspiring the common folk to virtue and letting this form the heart of the nation from the bottom up. Bjarni was fascinated by this approach, as he had always assumed Church leaders were the spiritual directors of a diocese. Thorlák had a very good point – particularly when the Church in Iceland was governed as much by chieftain policy as Canon Law.

Thorlák had particular interest in confession and penance. Being a scholar of Canon Law brought the reality of sin to the forefront in his mind. In Lincoln, it was strongly encouraged that each diocese developed a Penitential – that is, a book listing specific sins in great detail, along with the penance to be levied for each sin. Iceland, of course, had no such book; and if even if one did exist, it would not likely be well used. Bjarni and Thorlák pondered how they could hearten their parishioners toward greater virtue without explicit institutional norms to enforce these higher standards. Bjarni cautioned that, in his priestly experience, he found people tend toward one of two extremes when confronting sin: they either deny that higher standards apply to them, or they despair that they will never have the strength or desire to live more virtuously. Bjarni was determined to find a way to get parishioners to strive toward holiness without creating contention between the people and the Church.

Thorlák turned to the Victorine teachings on mercy, drawn from his study of *Decretum Ivo di Chartres* yet unfamiliar to most ordinary Catholics. Mercy was understood in scholarly terms but not readily applied to the people in their parishes. St. Augustine's story depicted mercy exactly well, but he was a mythical figure, unknown to most Icelanders. He not only lived centuries ago in a world far removed, but people felt his triumph over sin was proof of his greatness of mind – not something achievable among ordinary laborers.

Thorlák brought up Hugh of St. Victor's premise that God loved humankind especially in our imperfections. That idea was so unexpected, and so imbued with hope, that it stayed fresh in Thorlák's mind. He described the concept to Bjarni as best he could, insisting that the people of the parish could neither fall into denial nor despair if only they could grasp the fullness of God's love for them exactly as they are. God sees people in totality. He knows each of us as who we are intended to be; and also at the stage we are now at, not yet there, but on the way. Put another way, God loves us as much as though we were already our best selves – and, if we allow Him, he will help us get there.

It took a few explanations before Bjarni comprehended the idea. Once he understood, he imagined how that might be taught to the people in their parish. Thorlák suggested they start very simply, using a custom he had observed at the Abbey of St. Victor. When hearing confessions, he and Bjarni would enumerate the sinful behaviors of their penitents, and then assign specific penances for each instance. Then, they would explicitly take on that debt themselves, freeing penitents from the burden of reparation. The priests would assign the penances, emphasizing accountability for wrongdoing, but then perform the penances for them in a demonstration of God's mercy. It is a very powerful message to have a debt paid in full, especially when nothing has been done to deserve it. This gesture by the priests would hopefully surprise penitents to such a degree they would feel inspired to strive toward better living, rather than falling back on their sinful habits.

Bjarni loved this idea. Together, they set it in motion, to the utter astonishment of their parishioners. Penitents were completely disarmed by this unprecedented act of oblation by the very ones who could rightfully lord their moral superiority over them. Talk spread quickly about this startling practice. Those who grudgingly tolerated confession eagerly told their friends how wonderful this new experience was, to be freed from sin and given the opportunity to strive toward true holiness. Listeners were skeptical: Confession, the heavy yoke of obedience, the iron chains of bondage by the Church – a wonderful thing?

It was, truly, wonderful. Thorlák and Bjarni took the early morning hours to fulfill the prayer-penances of their people, finding such joy that they woke earlier and earlier as the summer went on, which was not difficult when the northern sun barely set at all. The spiritual benefits spread among the people like moss growing across the lava plains – a slow, subtle carpet of grace that was not at all ostentatious but a steady new growth enlivening the everyday landscape.

The years Thorlák spent at Kirkjubær were his happiest. It was a time of becoming that person he felt God intended him to be, and it echoed the words of his heavenly messenger as it fulfilled his longing to be a provider to a family. Could there, indeed, be a better bride than the Holy Catholic Church, the Bride of Christ? And, for his bride, he cultivated and harvested holiness from the very ground up. By 1168, the church at Kirkjubær was considered holy land throughout Iceland. Wise men said of Kirkjubær that there was *"nowhere more promising to find that man best fitted to carry the heaviest burden in Iceland."* It was an interesting remark, not without prophetic foreshadowing, but not yet to be fully revealed. As Thorlák concluded his sixth year at Kirkjubær, it likely occurred to him that he had once more experienced a time of creation, and might be approaching a time of completion.

A wealthy landowner, Thorkell Geirason, was one of the wise men who wondered about this priest of Kirkjubær with such a reputation for virtue. Thorkell was the householder of the second-wealthiest farmstead in the Diocese of Skálholt on an expansive tract of land in Álftaver. He was growing older and considering what he wanted his legacy to be. Surveying his farmstead, he saw prosperity and productivity – two excellent accomplishments in a land as fickle and unforgiving as Iceland. Yet he felt haunted by the Gospel passage from Matthew:

Lay not up to yourselves treasures on earth:
where the rust, and moth consume,
and where thieves break through and steal.
But lay up to yourselves treasures in heaven:
where neither the rust nor moth doth consume,
and where thieves do not break through, nor steal.
For where thy treasure is, there is thy heart also.

Thorkell could not stop thinking about the remarkable parish to the east. He heard they had transformed ordinary people in an ordinary district into something extraordinary, a bit of heaven on earth, with only the modest things they had. His farm, people said, was extraordinary among farms in Iceland for prospering as it had… but what would become of it after he died? Would his kinfolk, his farmhands, carry on what he had begun? Would they continue to build up this treasury, here, on earth? Or would it die off, like so many other crops when seasons turned unfavorable

… like he eventually would, himself? What was he doing now, to lay up treasure in heaven?

The seasoned householder set out to make a visit to Kirkjubær. It was two days' journey, and when he arrived, he was well rewarded by the opportunity to meet exactly the man he had hoped to see.

Thorkell Geirason inquired at the Kirkjubær farmstead as to whom the parish priest might be. He was shown to Bjarni and Thorlák, who were working side by side a few yards away. Thorkell glanced at the two men, one older, one younger, and asked which of the two was the householder? Bjarni responded in greeting. Thorlák offered their visitor to sit down and have something to drink, and the three men spent the remainder of the afternoon conversing about many things. Thorkell was most interested to learn of Thorlák's background, but he held his thoughts for quite some time. Finally, Thorkell felt he had heard all he needed to know.

"Father Thorlák," he said at last. "It is a wonder that there are two monasteries in Hólar, but none in Skálholt. Have you not noticed this yourself?"

Thorlák answered. "It would be very beneficial if

Skálholt had its own monastery. The School at Oddi does much toward the formation of good men, but it cannot compare to the profit that a monastery would bring to our region."

Thorkell continued. "Is this what you intend to have here, Father? A monastery?"

Thorlák was puzzled. "No. Surely, this is no monastery. It is just we two, and the farmhands. It is not that sizeable a property."

"Then, would you consider assisting in the establishment of a monastery elsewhere in Skálholt, on a more suitable estate?"

Thorlák remained perplexed. "I have not heard that such an estate is available."

"That is because, until now, it has not been. Father Thorlák, I would like to offer my own estate, at Thykkvibær, for such purpose. I wish to bequeath my holdings to you, that you would become the *húsbóndi*. Or more precisely: the Abbot of the monastery which I intend for you to establish."

At this, Thorlák and Bjarni were both speechless. It was a daunting proposal, completely unexpected, yet magnificent to imagine. Thorkell waited patiently, allowing the men to consider the proposal before them and admiring the reverence – and humility – with which they both received this offer.

"Would Father Bjarni accompany me there?" asked Thorlák at last.

Bjarni interjected. "I could not! It would not be possible, Dear Father, for there would be no priest or householder here!"

The two men realized the immensity of the change dawning on the horizon of this proposal. "Father Thorlák," Bjarni continued dolefully, "you would be leaving Kirkjubær for greater things… as we both knew would happen one day."

Thorlák took a long, thoughtful pause, and then said, "I must pray. I must take this matter to prayer before all else. Then, of course, it must be drawn up before Bishop Klæng and approved by His Excellency. And then, there is the matter of who would populate this monastery. Are there sufficient men in Iceland desiring the monastic rule? These things must be considered before we can proceed."

Thorkell responded, "Of course. All will proceed with diligence and approval. I am confident this is

God's will for me and the property He has entrusted to my care. This is the legacy I am to leave as my treasury on earth, that I may begin now to store up treasure in heaven."

Thorlák was satisfied with this answer, though still quite unsettled with the suddenness of this turn of events. A glance toward Bjarni found his face with a similar expression, yet he said with much optimism, "Dear Thorlák, whatever God's will may be, let us pray for one another to have the strength and courage to face what is to come!"

Thorkell stayed the night, sharing more ideas over dinner about what he envisioned for this future monastery. The monasteries in Hólar were under Benedictine rule, but with Father Thorlák overseeing this effort; it would no doubt be an Augustinian community. Thorlák speculated his first step should be himself to formally adopt the Rule of Saint Augustine. This was a relatively simple matter, given that he had already been observant of the rule in nearly everything he was doing at Kirkjubær. He would present himself to Bishop Klæng as a follower of the Augustinian rule wishing to open this way of life to other priests in Skálholt. With enough interested men, a community of canons could be instituted. A "canon" was any diocesan priest who lived and worked in conjunction with the other priests; a "canon regular" was one who adhered to a specific rule of life, such as the Rule of St. Augustine. Thus, the men would earn the title "Canons Regular," and they would be welcome to occupy the farmstead at Thykkvibær as their common home.

The more the men discussed, the clearer it became that this plan had all the right players at just the right time. It was indeed an answer to many prayers, and a continuing fulfillment of Thorlák's formation. At night, Thorlák would pray Psalm 143, intending each word as though he himself had been the psalmist –

"Teach me to do thy will, for thou art my God.

Thy good spirit shall lead me into the right land."

The right land, right now, was that which was about to be bestowed to him, west of where he laid his head now but still a new land in every practical sense his home. He mused, too, that he had come to this "right land" by way of France and England… a wayward route providing the right instruction by the right men, for just the right way to bring the light of holiness to shine from within Iceland.

As *húsbóndi*, Thorlák could not only oversee the establishment of a Canon house, but he could fulfill his duty to provide for his family. His sisters would have an endowment from his income, and his mother could have a permanent home in the family name.

CHAPTER ELEVEN

THE HOUSE AT THYKKVIBÆR

With hearts swollen equally by hope for the future and pain of departure, Bjarni saw Thorlák off to his new endeavor in Álftaver. The two priests were deeply affected by their friendship and vowed that never a day would pass that one would not pray earnestly for the other. That evening, Bjarni stood at his friend's bed-space and, through tears, declared aloud, "This particular place will never again be equally well occupied if Thorlák does not occupy it himself!" Thorlák felt the same of him, volunteering his praises of Bjarni and Kirkjubær at every opportunity.

Now thirty five years old, Thorlák took the Rule of St. Augustine upon himself and felt the elation, the paradoxical *freedom*, of a man willingly bound for the rest of his life by a pledge of love… not unlike a husband (or, *húsbóndi*) to a bride of a higher order. His benefactor was true to his promise and provided everything Thorlák might need, from living quarters to livestock to monetary provisions for the incidentals they now had to consider – such as the attire proper to the Canons Regular of St.

Augustine. The vestments consisted of white robe and black cape, and other supplies, such as books and candles, were obtained in quantities estimated to serve fifteen men. Right now, it was only Thorlák and Thorkell, but once the house had been properly established and approved by Bishop Klæng, they hoped to attract at least ten others with accommodations left for visitors. Books and candles would need to be sent for from the European continent. Candles were rarely found in Iceland outside the few churches that already had them, for bees to make the wax cannot survive that harsh of a climate. On the other hand, oil lamps were plentiful but not proper for worship.

Thorkell had definite ambitions for Thorlák to lead the affairs of the monastery. His immediate wish, though, was to have for himself a taste of the same heaven-on-earth the people had in Kirkjubær – and so, he requested that he be admitted as one of the Canons of the monastery. Thorlák explained carefully that this was not an appointed position, but rather, a state in life for which one must first be properly disposed and properly formed. His benefactor pleaded his case, promising his desire was earnest and that he would take every necessary step to see this to fruition. Thorlák was impressed and agreed to admit Thorkell into the first group of candidates for monastic residence.

As each day progressed, the needs and duties became readily apparent, as easily as if this had all been conceived and prescribed far in advance and he were simply the one to carry out the plans. They spent a good many hours drawing up the constitution of the monastery in anticipation of presenting this to Bishop Klæng. Thorlák was meticulous in his writing, attentive to the finest details and careful to consider fully every aspect proper to establishing a house of Canons.

There was little need to worry. Bishop Klæng was enthusiastic about the idea from the moment he sat down with Thorlák. Klæng was a very active man as Bishop of Skálholt. As Icelanders have the unique geographic capability of standing with one foot on the Eurasian continental plate and one foot on the North American plate in the rift valley at Thingvellir, so it seemed Klæng stood somewhere between the worldly materialism of his reputation and the ascetic holiness his heart desired. He was widely known for throwing lavish parties and bestowing the finest foods on his guests, and he adorned the Bishop's estate with finery purchased from all parts of Scandinavia and Northern Europe. On the other hand, he adopted many penitential practices, such as depriving himself of shoes and outer clothing – which are particularly harsh disciplines in a climate and terrain such as Iceland. He was a bit of an enigma, garnering support across several prominent clans rather than casting loyalties with any one of the *goðar* – yet he retained close ties with Gizur Hallsson, keeping him close at hand as an advisor on the social and political matters of the Diocese. Klæng's main goal was to grow the Catholic Church in Iceland, and to him, this meant elevating the experience above that of a weekly gathering at a farmstead church. If the Church represented the Kingdom of God, Klæng felt the people ought to associate Catholicism with the lavish splendor and aesthetics found among the nobility.

A monastery in the Diocese of Skálholt, particularly one modeled after the Victorines in Paris, would be a tremendous asset. It would increase the holiness of the priests in the diocese and establish a presence that would be recognized all over Europe. Who could say – maybe men from the continent would be attracted to Iceland, and would bring their material wealth with them! Klæng gave his hearty support and approval. The monastery at Thykkvibær was officially established, and now, the task at hand was to fill the monastery with good men.

On the monastery's charter, Thorlák listed himself as Prior, since he was the only priest at this point. With books and vestments arriving from abroad, he could begin instruction to any priests who wished to join their community. Eventually, Bishop Klæng would consecrate one of the men Abbot of the monastery and their community would be fully operational.

Word spread quickly, between Klæng's prolific social gatherings and plain talk among people in the region. Thorlák, too, assisted in recruiting by inviting anyone at Oddi to consider joining the newly formed house as Canons Regular of St. Augustine. The Oddaverjar were very pleased with this opportunity. They, too, saw the great advantages of having a monastery in the spirit of St. Victor right here in Iceland. Students being sent to study in Paris could return home to further their formation, and in kind, the monastery would benefit greatly from the collective wisdom of those who had been educated by the Victorines. It was also quite obvious to them that this was a fertile center for advancing the influence of the Oddaverjar throughout Iceland. Perhaps, they mused, the next Bishop would represent the Oddaverjar instead of the Haukadelir clan. Perhaps this next Bishop would come from the monastery itself.

And so it was that the Augustinian Canons Regular began thriving in southern Iceland on the former farmstead-turned-monastery at Thykkvibær. Thorlák's formation of the men there was exceptional. As he had at Kirkjubær, Thorlák managed to take the most complex theological principles on *caritas* and the Sacraments and present them in a way that was relevant and relatable. His instruction was equally suitable to parish priests as it was to theological scholars. With the rhythm of the canonical hours, the prescribed periods of labor, the high standards of conduct and the constant reminder that *"where two or three gather in Jesus' name, God is present,"* Thorlák generated a harmonious lifestyle which resonated all through Iceland and beyond. The monastery attracted many visitors from all over Europe, as had been Bishop Klæng's hope, and each remarked on the profound holiness surrounding the entire estate. Thorlák incorporated two more aspects into the ordinary Canonical living of the Augustinians, drawn from his observations at St. Victor and his study of the Victorine writings on mysticism. He instituted *preferential silence*, by which Canons were encouraged to refrain from speaking whenever possible. This cultivated a greater awareness of the sacred in ordinary doings by giving men the space in which to contemplate as they work. Secondly, Thorlák limited travel to only that which was absolutely necessary, requiring permission by the Prior. He devised this as a living demonstration of St. Augustine's premise, *"Our hearts are restless until they rest in YOU, My God."* Restricting the freedom to wander brought the ordinary inclinations toward restlessness to the forefront of the Canons' awareness and permitted them to rightly order their yearnings toward God. Visitors were especially struck by the aptitude of Thorlák's initiatives, remarking as many had before that his genius reached far beyond his actual years — which, by now, were 37.

That year, the Canons – including Thorkell, who was now fully vested himself – voted to elect from among themselves the Abbot of their monastery. To nobody's surprise, by unanimous decision, the honor went to Thorlák. He found this almost painful to accept, even though he had been Prior for many months now. His heart was very much invested in the entire community and he did not feel superior to his fellow Canons in any way. To him, they were a reflection of the Apostles, none greater than the other and each bestowed with unique gifts to bring to the body as a whole. The other Canons saw Thorlák as much more than a brother. He was to them a spiritual father – even though he was younger than some Canons by decades. He led them firmly and gently, with judiciousness and genuine care for their souls. He nourished them, body and spirit, and provided for them in every way a father might. Without realizing it, Thorlák had fully matured into the man he worried he might never become.

When six years passed, Thorlák wondered if he would mark another time of completion. Here was his vocation, fulfilled. He was priest, *húsbondi*, provider for his mother and sisters, and Abbot of the first monastery in the Diocese of Skálholt. As far as Thorlák was concerned, he had found his bride, and he was the happiest of bridegrooms.

CHAPTER TWELVE

THE RISE OF THE ODDAVERJAR

The monastic life provided insulation from the turmoil of the outside world. The year was 1174, but within the walls of Thykkvibær, time was marked only by canonical hours of prayer. Jón Loftsson, age 50, had attained prominence as Iceland's most powerful chieftain and had a reputation as a "peacemaker" – that is, one who diplomatically settled disputes between often violently angry individuals. Each case he settled won him great favor, if not great numbers of people who were indebted to his rulings. Thorlák had little to do with Jón but kept close ties with Páll, his and Ragnheið's son. Páll, now a fine young man of eighteen, was bright as his uncle and ambitious as his father. He had the benefit of an Oddi education and many hours of instruction with his Uncle Thorlák, discussing spiritual matters and the finer points of Canon Law. Thorlák was terribly fond of Páll, making little effort to hide his affection for the boy and making time night or day to assist him whenever he needed anything. Páll certainly knew his father and spent hours with him, too; but Thorlák asserted his role as foster-father as much as doting uncle. He may have sought to counteract the moral disregard shown by Jón with a double portion of instruction in virtue – yet the fondness between the two was genuine, and it was obvious that Páll looked up to his Uncle Thorlák with great love and respect. Páll filled the place in Thorlák's heart that longed for children, and indeed, he treated his bright-eyed nephew with as much love as his own son might have received.

Thorlák asked Páll if he felt that the priesthood was in his future. In truth, Páll was more interested in law than religion. Still, he felt the two were closely interconnected. Civil law could not exist without willingness to put the good of others before themselves, which, in essence, was the core of Christian faith. Thorlák urged Páll to consider Canon Law, suggesting it would be worthwhile study given his propensity for politics and would afford many advantages in working with the Bishops of Iceland. To wit, Jón Loftsson formed a powerful alliance with Gizur Hallsson, uniting two clans in their focus on the Bishop's seat in Skálholt. Bishop Klæng entertained members of both clans with great regularity and magnanimity.

The many guests of Bishop Klæng began to wonder if his ascetic habits were taking a toll on his health. He had developed recurring infections in the soles of his feet, injured by traveling barefoot across the Icelandic terrain. Ordinary congestion in his throat and chest were made worse by not protecting himself from the driving winds and soaking rains when he ventured out. He might have recovered without incident if he had rested or eased up on his self-imposed penances; however, each infection had not enough time to fully heal before the next took hold. It was a gradual decline, but a decline in his health nonetheless, and was noticeable by those in his company.

Thorlák heard of Bishop Klæng's situation and urged his Canons to pray for these difficulties to be resolved. When he himself prayed this intention, he felt an uneasy sense about him. It was not so much the Bishop's declining health as it was a persistent feeling that he was being summoned. There were no words to describe this feeling, just an unflagging impression of something beyond the horizon that he could not yet see, but would know when it arrived. He felt the need to prepare for whatever it might be.

The Icelandic National Assembly was a few weeks away, and anyone in Iceland was welcome to attend. Common folk would congregate in the fields of Thingvellir while the *Althing* convened to discuss matters of law and civic decision, to settle disputes, and allow the Bishop a forum to declare any revisions to the Church calendar and regulations. This year, people speculated with increasing certainty that Bishop Klæng would call for an election to name his successor, such was the rapid downturn in his health, with no hopeful sign of recovery.

Did Thorlák know the extent of Bishop Klæng's declining health? Was he made privy to the thinking of his mentors among the Oddaverjar? Did Páll discuss his father's intentions when Uncle Thorlák visited? Or did Divine Providence whisper directly to Thorlák's heart in a voice so clear and sweet that he simply could not resist it?

History has not recorded exactly what unfolded. What we do know is that Jón Loftsson thought it would be advantageous to nominate an Oddaverjar-backed candidate to replace Bishop Klæng, and, at the same time, Thorlák felt an uncharacteristically strong inclination to make the journey to the

Althing, even as he still discouraged unnecessary traveling among the Canons. By the time the *Althing* was ready to convene, there were three candidates to be presented for Bishop of Skálholt. Two were prominent names among the diocese: Páll Sölvason, a priest/chieftain from Reykholt who was well acquainted with Jón Loftsson; and Ogmund Kálfsson, recently consecrated abbot of the monastery on Flatey, a mile-long island off mainland Iceland's Westfjord region. Ogmund and Thorlák were well acquainted as Thorlák lent his assistance to getting this monastery up and running much as he had done at the inception of Thykkvibær's House of Canons. Flatey's, too, was an Augustinian monastery approved by Bishop Klæng after seeing the success of Thorlák's monastery at Thykkvibær.

The third man was nominated by Jón Loftsson himself. We do not know if he was aware of Jón's intentions. Most hearing the third nomination were familiar with this man by name but had never met him personally, and were therefore skeptical of his worthiness for office.

The third nominee was: Thorlák Thórhallsson, Abbot of Thykkvibær.

CHAPTER THIRTEEN

ELECTION AT THE ALTHING

The proceedings of the Althing turned to the oratorical contest between Abbot Ogmund and Séra Páll, each of whom sought to convince Bishop Klæng of his suitability to succeed him. Klæng searched each man carefully to discern which had the right combination of connection and experience to best take on the operations of the Diocese. Ogmund's curriculum vitae was impressive. He had good education and strong administrative skills. He was well qualified as Abbot; however, it was unclear what his vision would be for the Diocese. Klæng could attest to his solid moral character. Ogmund would be a good and fair manager of financial affairs. He spoke of his wish for a unification of purpose among the clergy, hearkening to the European impetus to standardize practices and devotions throughout the entire Church. Unity was a good thing to strive toward, especially in a diocese where married priests put the interests of their own families first, posing many a conflict of interest with the others in their parishes.

Séra Páll, on the other hand, *was* a married priest
with two sons and two daughters. He, however,
was a chieftain in his district, and therefore more
politically savvy and better connected than many
priests. He showed a keen sense for handling
disputes and rendering fair decisions in complicated
business matters. If Diocesan growth was the goal,
Páll would be the man to choose. Klæng could
easily envision several new buildings and property
holdings consecrated for Diocesan use, with
wealthy landowners to carry the burden of upkeep.
Páll's was one of the larger districts northwest of
Skálholt; Klæng had no doubt he could manage the
affairs of the Diocese without difficulty. Of the
two candidates, Séra Páll was the superior orator by
far. Ogmund, however, had a more even-tempered
sensibility about him, suggesting that his diplomacy
might go further than Páll's vaunting style.

The two men carried the proceedings from morning
well into the late afternoon. With Iceland's summer
sun affording unlimited daylight, the assembly could
easily extend into the next day, if such were needed.
There was a brief adjournment before the Bishop's
candidates would take questions from those among
the assembly, when none other than Gizur Hallsson

stood at the speaker's stage and made the following
inquiry:

"Your Excellency! Was it not the case that there
were three men put forth as nominees to the office
of Bishop of Skálholt?"

A hush crept over the gathering as Bishop Klæng
responded from his seat with a grand nod of his
head.

Gizur continued: "Then I must ask of you, Your
Excellency: Where, indeed, is the third man
nominated to this office?"

The crowd began to murmur. Klæng sat, silently,
while the other candidates quickly ascended to the
speaker's platform in rapid response.

"If he is here, he has not shown himself all day!
This is quite suspect!" began Séra Páll.

"I am familiar with Abbot Thorlák," asserted
Ogmund, "but not sufficiently to vouch for his
peculiar absence."

Gizur interjected, "If this is the nominee of Jón
Loftsson, he is no doubt a man of good standing.
Perhaps he has been detained, or has fallen ill?"

The crowd's voices steadily rose until Klæng himself implored the assembly, "Does not any man here have any testimony to the character of Abbot Thorlák Thórhallsson? Let him speak, who is well acquainted with Thorlák!"

A brief pause was followed by Séra Páll making the following statement: "If I may lend my opinion, Your Excellency, I would be most reluctant to have the likes of this Thorlák, of whom we have heard in legend only, at the helm of any Diocese. He may have a splendid reputation as a man of holiness, but his absence surely calls his character into serious doubt."

In a sudden appearance from the crowd, a frantic Jón Loftsson pushed his way onto the speaker's platform. "I am at a loss to explain this peculiar turn of events. I have known Thorlák since his earliest childhood, and what I can only conclude is that we are seeing the bedevilment of an ineptitude arising from a speech impediment which has tormented him his entire life. Although I can, and do, vouch for the might of his intellect and the shrewdness of his ideas, I must concede that a man who cannot speak is not fit for an office such as Bishop. It was my sincere hope that Thorlák had conquered this handicap; yet, it seems, it has overtaken him in a dreadful and telling relapse."

The assembly had much to say among themselves about this puzzling turn of events. Then, another man rose and ascended the speaker's platform with great urgency.

"Fellow Icelanders!"

The crowd grew silent.

"I must appeal to you on behalf of my friend, my superior, and my fellow Canon Regular, Abbot Thorlák."

Several present recognized this man by face, but not by the white robe and black cape he now wore daily. This was the wealthy farmsteader from Álftaver who sought out Thorlák back when he was still a parish priest in Siða. This was –

"My name is Thorkell Geirason. I am a Canon Regular of Saint Augustine under the direction of Abbot Thorlák. It is my property on which the monastery of Thykkvibær has been under his supervision for six years. I will vouch that Abbot Thorlák has every qualification to be a magnificent Bishop. He is disciplined, sharp, even-tempered and resourceful. He is loyal, diligent and faithful to his religious duties. Likewise, he is a dedicated laborer, a skilled planner and a meticulous manager of finances. He leads men like brothers, gently but firmly, speaking only when necessary. It is a sign of monastic obedience that Thorlák has not spoken as yet, for the words I have heard today have been largely extraneous, redundant and self-aggrandizing. On the contrary: Thorlák strives to *do* everything best rather than talk most!"

Thorkell pointed squarely at a man in the assembly, standing off to the side, dressed in the same habit as himself. "There!" said Thorkell. "There is the sixth Bishop of Skálholt!"

He stepped down, and applause began to rise from the crowd. Bishop Klæng stood and summoned the silent abbot forward. Thorlák reluctantly complied, ascending the speaker's stage to an ever-increasing ovation. When the clapping subsided, Thorlák faced the assembly.

After a long pause, he said:

"Your Excellency: In deciding which man of the three should be your successor, I commend to you the following words from the Psalmist, King David:

'Blessed is the man who does not walk in step with the wicked, or stand in the way that sinners take, or sit in the company of mockers;

'But, whose delight is in the law of the Lord, and who meditates on his law day and night. That man is like a tree, planted by streams of water, which yields its fruit in season, and whose leaf does not wither — whatever he does, prospers.' "

With a nod of reverence toward Bishop Klæng, Thorlák descended the platform and returned to his former place in the crowd. The other two candidates stood, silently, too puzzled to speak. Bishop Klæng glanced about as he mused on what had transpired.

The assembly concluded that the matter of selecting a successor to Bishop Klæng would be deferred until the following day. The crowd began to disperse, hungry and thirsty and filled with opinion and chatter. Thorlák retreated with Thorkell to where the two were staying that night. Whatever happened, he entrusted all to Divine Providence. Something had nudged him interiorly to journey here in the first place. If his role was only to remind the other two candidates of their right priorities, his work here was complete, and he took good satisfaction in that.

The following day, it was decided that Bishop Klæng would select his successor by his own decision, rather than popular opinion. The very thought of another day of oratorical posturing seemed exhausting and, frankly, fruitless.

Klæng did not take long to arrive at his decision. With assistance, he ascended to the speaker's platform, gingerly enduring the pain from his afflicted and bandaged feet.

"As the Fifth Bishop of Skálholt, I bestow the title of Bishop-Electus to the man who will succeed me in office…

Thorlák Thórhallson, the wise Abbot of Thykkvibær."

CHAPTER FOURTEEN

BISHOP ELECTUS

"From everyone who has been given much, much will be demanded; and from the one who has been entrusted with much, much more will be asked." (Luke 12:48)

The events following Bishop Klæng's announcement rushed upon Thorlák like a cascade. Those around him saw a man standing with his head erect, his palms upturned, and an expression of calm readiness. He looked like one anticipating a gale; or, perhaps, a great feast, with the countenance of a host who is both pleased to commence and mindful of every detail.

The people nearest him offered immediate congratulations which he accepted with cordial acknowledgment. Jón Loftsson, beaming, embraced his shoulders and declared, "At last, you and I are truly brothers, in every purpose!" As though forgetting his detraction from the day before, Jón added, "The right decision has been made."

Thorlák recalled with regret that Jón's uncle and his foster-father, Eyjólfur, had died while Thorlák was studying in Lincoln. He took a breath in reverence of blessed memory, bringing him present in mind for this moment which he owed, in every way, to Eyjólfur's guiding hands.

Thorlák responded, "It is the wish of Divine Providence that we work toward the betterment of one another, indeed."

Thorlák received attention, congratulation, scrutiny and exhortation from people of great and ordinary standing alike. Many simply wished to see this man for themselves, having heard the name but never seeing Thorlák in person. Thorkell helped form a receiving line to ease the pressing of the crowd, which was beginning to show worry on his friend's brow.

At last he was summoned by Gizur Hallsson informing him that Bishop Klæng would like to see him apart from the assembly to discuss the matters pertaining to the transfer of the office.

Some of the details were straightforward. Thorlák would return to his Canonry and continue his daily functions while Klæng prepared for the transition at the Bishop's Estate in Skálholt. The pertinent matters needing immediate attention would be handled by Gizur Hallsson. Provisions also needed to be made for Thorlák's formal consecration in Norway, as Iceland was under the Archbishopric of Trondheim, headed at that time by the devout future saint Eysteinn Erlendsson. All of these details could be clarified over the next several months, and the transition would likely be a gradual one. Klæng appreciated that Thorlák was so widely reputed to be compliant and easy to work with. He also took confidence in having established a formal tie now with the Oddaverjar and therefore the majority ruling clan of Iceland. Things looked like they were headed forward on a steady path for the Diocese of Skálholt.

Thorlák would use this period to appoint his replacement as Abbot and help the Canons at Thykkvibær change hands. He would divide his time between Thykkvibær and Skálholt to familiarize himself with the needs and operations of the Diocese as well as the men he would be working with. Thorlák would also attend to any personal affairs, making provisions for his own family to transition with him.

Halla, Thorlák's mother, was overjoyed by this turn of events. Her own health had weakened in her 74th year but she was as strong in spirit as ever before. She rightfully boasted that she had always known her son would go on to be someone remarkable in this world, and she praised God that she had been permitted to live long enough to see for herself. She could not have been happier or more proud of her only son. In these days, time almost seemed to stop for her, right there in the serene light of Thykkvibær, this holy ground where the trials of the past were out of reach and anxiety for the future was nonexistent. All was just as it should be, in God's designs, unfurling before her eyes.

Yet still, being Thorlák's mother, she soon learned of the plans underway and issued a firm order to her son: "As I live, you are not to endanger your life or mine by journeying to Norway! Sooner should you let the Archbishop come to you than place your future and my wellbeing in peril!"

Her apprehension reflected the tension between Iceland and Norway which had begun two years earlier. Mounting hostilities between the two countries led to frequent ambush and threats of death, particularly toward priests, at the hands of impulsive and vengeful combatants on both sides. The acrimony between the nations began with an unfortunate incident in 1172 where a Norwegian sailor on business in Iceland became involved in a dispute with an Icelandic priest. In the course of their argument, the priest's house caught fire (or, was set ablaze, depending on who tells the story) and burned to the ground. Blinded by anger, the priest set out to avenge his loss. He found a Norwegian ship at dock and set it on fire, destroying it. The story goes that this ship belonged to a different man altogether, and with this act of wanton injustice, a bitter feud erupted between the two countries. With every retelling, events became more and more inflamed in the minds of those offended, with threats of death swapped furiously between the two countries. It was a tenuous time for an Icelandic priest to travel to Norway. To complicate the picture further, it was necessary for the Archbishop in Niðaros to seek the King's approval of anyone appointed to authority – including national enemies. It was a risky time, to be sure, but Thorlák knew his mother's apprehension was not fear of ambush. As she increased in years, she had begun showing the

ordinary signs of frailty. Her step was not very
steady and she was easily winded. Though strong in
words, Halla was uneasy about being left alone. She
worried what would happen if Thorlák were
detained, or attacked, or perished at sea. What
would become of her, in her failing strength,
without Thorlák close at hand? She never
articulated these thoughts, but the closeness
between mother and son permitted Thorlák these
insights intuitively. Out of deference first to his
mother's need, and then a measure of good
prudence, he decided it best to wait to make the
journey to Norway, and assured Halla of his
decision.

Even without a formal consecration, Thorlák would
assume the title Bishop-Electus, affording him
nearly every privilege a Bishop might have in terms
of administration, arbitration and jurisdiction. He
was in a very good position to take over the See of
Skálholt when Bishop Klæng was ready to step
down.

The weeks passed quickly. While Thorlák
meticulously settled affairs at the monastery, Klæng
intended to do the same at Skálholt. He had
accomplished a great deal in his 23 years as Bishop.

He and Gizur Hallsson oversaw construction of a new cathedral church in Skálholt, built of the finest Norwegian wood and adorned with an exquisite gold, gem-studded altar chalice. The books, too, had been specially commissioned for the new church. Klæng prided himself on teaching priests the proper way to sing the psalms and purchased new psalters for this purpose.

Bishop Klæng kept in regular contact with Archbishop Eysteinn of Norway; the latter, sending both cordial greetings and pastoral letters of exhortation as is proper to his office. Archbishop Eysteinn promoted the Victorine vision of encouraging people to strive toward higher virtue. He sent a letter in 1173 imploring the priests of Iceland to speak out against the promiscuity for which Iceland was becoming notorious among the other nations in Europe. He also wanted to see more faithful conformity to Catholic norms across all in his Archbishopric. He knew Iceland considered itself exempt from European customs, but Eysteinn reminded that the Church was not mere fashion; it was the Kingdom of God to which all owe fidelity. Perhaps these exhortations drove Klæng to shed his shoes in reparation for the sins of himself and his people, ignoring all the warning signs and manifestations of frostbite which he accepted as his own brand of stigmata, but which ultimately shortened his life and reign as Bishop.

Whether from habit or failing health, Klæng increased his spending past the level of income received by the tithe and by contributions from benefactors. Gizur Hallsson implored him to curtail his extravagance to no avail. It came to pass that the Diocese's greatest patron, the Haukadelir clan, ceased all contributions in an attempt to send a more direct message. Klæng did not flinch. He exploited his ties with the Oddaverjar and relied on their contributions instead, and he incurred a great deal of debt along with magnanimous words and lofty promises.

Thorlák was increasingly apprised of the financial affairs of the Diocese by both Gizur and members of the Oddaverjar. Jón Loftsson, with frequent trips to Norway and status as nobility there, kept Thorlák up on affairs overseas. Thorlák became familiar with the diplomatic relationship between Skálholt and other Dioceses, in Europe and at home in Hólar. He listened closely and observed Jón with a touch of wonderment. The charismatic chieftain was an influential leader who not only commanded attention but always seemed to come out ahead in his transactions. And there was what distinguished Jón from others: he was highly focused on *transactions*. You could almost palpably feel Jón's appraisal of your value to him in every interaction. When Jón saw value in you or your contribution, he was solicitous and generous. When your offering was not to his standard, he moved past you just as quickly as though you had vanished, or never existed. He did not subsist on relationships; he lived through *transactions*.

It was all the more reason Thorlák felt compelled to be a father-figure to Páll, who was now a student in Lincoln and showing great achievement there. Jón and his relatives taught Páll very well in the skills of the mind. Thorlák was determined to teach him the skills of the heart. Jón taught Páll how to be strong; Thorlák sought to teach him how to be vulnerable. Secretly, Páll loved his uncle fiercely, feeling like he was the only one among the entire Oddaverjar who truly knew Páll as a person, not as simply another protégé. His mother did not pay much attention to anything he did with Thorlák. Ragnheið's loyalty was completely with Jón, and everything she did came back to the same premise: "You must make your family proud because you are the great-grandson of the King of Norway!"

Sometimes, Páll just wanted to be a boy, growing up in Iceland. He got to do that when Uncle Thorlák visited. In fact, every time Páll passed a wild daisy, he smiled to himself, recalling the day his uncle had explained theology to him using the flower with the hardy bloom more often found underfoot than adorning any altar. This, Thorlák began, was the Kingdom of God. It can grow anywhere God wishes, even in hostile climates, even where volcanic ash has left a bitter trail. It grows wherever God sees the need. And, it needs in return. These daisies need to be seen, and loved, if they are to be daisies and not overgrowth. They are simple, yet intricate. They do not require lavish portions to live well. And when they bloom, they are each a tiny monstrance of thanksgiving to the God who gave them life.

Thorlák had touched the daisies as he spoke, and Páll thought he saw them respond. When his uncle finished talking, he looked quietly into Páll's eyes with his own, blue as the Arctic and brimming with love. He recalled that moment feeling like something had been planted deep within his own heart: a seed of something, which Páll wanted to be sure not to neglect.

Thorlák had that effect on people. Páll was not the only one who noticed. Many people from surrounding farms told stories of the "miracle man" at the monastery who would come and pray over sick livestock, imparting healing almost immediately. One man claimed his barn was on fire and the Abbot cast a prayer over it, sprinkled it with holy water, and extinguished the blaze immediately with no trace of damage. Thorlák never spoke of these things and none of the Canons Regular repeated these stories, but word traveled well among those who witnessed them.

At Christmastime, in 1175, a group of visitors urgently knocked at the doors of Thykkvibær, calling for the Bishop-Elect. Klæng's health had taken a very sudden turn, and Thorlák was needed immediately. He gathered his belongings and summoned his Augustinian brothers about him. Thorlák gave a brief farewell, asking his fellow Canons to pray for him always, to forgive him for his shortcomings, and to continue seeking holiness in all they did. He handed his ceremonial Abbot's crozier to the man who would succeed him, conferring his stole on his shoulders and announcing to the group, "This man is now your Spiritual Father; listen to him!" Thorlák kept the white robe and black cape he wore every day, telling those in his party that he may be on the road to the Bishop's Estate, but he would be an Augustinian wherever he went, and it was of greatest importance to maintain dress proper to one's office.

The most difficult moment came when Thorlák embraced his mother, feeling her arms about his neck and inhaling the scent of her hair deeply as he kissed her goodbye, hearing her whisper, *"Ég Elska Thig!"* He promised her a very special place in the Bishop's mansion, and she smiled at the illustration her imagination created. Thorlák had a sense that this promise would be fulfilled quite differently than she envisioned, and he was correct. Before she could take up residence with her son in Skálholt, Halla died peacefully in her sleeping quarters at Thykkvibær. The brothers arranged a beautiful, reverent funeral to honor the woman who faithfully encouraged her son to the greatness of his destiny. Páll, being in Europe, missed his grandmother's burial; his brother Örm attended, and Jón Loftsson was there as a representative of the Oddaverjar and stood with the other *goðar* in attendance. Ragnheið, Eyvǫr and Örm sat in a place of honor while their brother, Bishop-Electus Thorlák, presided at both Mass and burial. Had Bishop Klæng been well enough, he too would have been in attendance; however, it was not long before his own funeral was prepared in Skálholt.

On February 28, 1176, Bishop Klæng Thorsteinsson died in his sickbed at Skálholt. In the days following the funeral, the Solemn Mass of Conferral was held at the Cathedral in Skálholt, presided by Bishop Brand Sæmundsson of Hólar, to inaugurate the next Bishop of Skálholt. Jón Loftsson was present and spoke at both ceremonies, highly praising Bishop Klæng's legacy and promising many greater achievements to come with Bishop Thorlák at the helm.

The ivory crozier was passed, like a torch, to the white-gloved hand awaiting it. The cathedral resounded with applause as Thorlák bowed to receive the miter of his office. And, with that, Thorlák Thórhallsson became the Sixth Bishop of Skálholt.

CHAPTER FIFTEEN

JOURNEY AND CONSECRATION

Though he missed his mother terribly, Thorlák now had full liberty to travel to Norway in spite of the ongoing feud, which had many still wishing he would defer travel until relations improved. He asserted it was futile to wait any longer, and with his authority now as Bishop, his desire meant action even when his advisors disagreed. The two men with whom he worked most closely were Jón Loftsson and Gizur Hallsson, whom he commissioned to make arrangements for his voyage. Gizur began assembling an extensive entourage, insisting that a large contingency would afford better protection from ambush. Jón, the frequent guest of Norwegian royalty, considered which gifts should be brought first to the Archbishop, and then to King Magnús V. Wool and cloth tapestry would suit the Archbishop, while narwhal ivory and wild gyrfalcons were gifts better fit for royalty.

Bishop Thorlák firmly disagreed in both matters.

He saw no purpose to a large entourage, asserting that he did not feel the danger warranted taking extra men at extra expense to serve no purpose other than to stand by. He lambasted the notion of plying the King and Archbishop with material goods. Thorlák stated that the Catholic Church possessed the *thesaurus ecclesiae*, the treasury of merits of Jesus Christ and all the Holy Saints. Praying the Holy Mass for the monarchy and each of its members, and likewise for Archbishop Eysteinn, would have infinitely more value than any ivory tusk would bring, and would send the proper message befitting that of a Spiritual Shepherd. A Bishop bearing material gifts teaches that respect is derived from a man's goods, rather than originating in his character. Thorlák neither wanted to disrespect his hosts nor overshadow his genuine need for their acceptance by distracting them with gifts.

Jón began lecturing his Bishop as though he were still a student at Oddi. "Thorlák, you need to remember," he began, "this is not your monastery. The treasury of merits may be a wonderful image in the world to come, but in this world, there are people with royal office whose actual treasuries could purchase our entire country, if they so desired. You are naïve if you expect a king to find your meager offer of prayer of any greater worth than if I were to perform *galdur* for his entertainment!"

Thorlák leveled his glance at Jón and replied, "Put not your trust in princes, nor in the sons of men, who cannot save; when their breath departs, they return to the earth."

Growing impatient, Jón shouted, "For as long as I live, I will never understand the *galdur* you have over my family, Thorlák Thórhallsson! You possess not even half the wit of a chieftain! You can barely speak for yourself, and when you do, you spout psalms like utter nonsense!"

Unimpressed, Thorlák responded, "Unless you can justify any of these excessive expenditures, given the magnitude of the deficit facing this Diocese, I will be traveling with one assistant, and with no additional material goods than are necessary for the voyage." After a pause, he added: "And, Jón: You shall address your Bishop as *Your Excellency*."

Jón became livid. Gizur held up a hand to try and stop him, but Jón's temper had the best of him.

"You would not even have that title if it were not for me! You would do very well to recall who gave you a respectable reputation when even your own father could not!"

Thorlák quietly asked, "As respectable a reputation as you have given my sister?"

At this, Gizur had to physically restrain Jón, who lunged toward Thorlák with blind rage. "If you will not let me do it, then let him go to Norway and be killed!" Jón screamed. "I will surely make it known that he represents every spite-filled priest on this island, and let him take the full wrath of the Norwegians so that this dispute and this imbecile Bishop may both be done away with!"

Gizur rebuked Thorlák, "It is shameful that you provoke his temper as you do!" He managed to escort Jón out of the room and then to the outer courtyard. His epithets could still be heard in venomous succession.

Thorlák stood, alone, in thought. He knew this first battle as Bishop was only the prelude of many more ahead. Jón was right about one thing: This was not his monastery. His ideas were not the kind that men here sought after. He recalled the words of his old friend Bjarni, about those who did not take well to the mention of virtue, and felt a leaden weight overtake his shoulders. He was indeed that man who would carry the heaviest burdens of Iceland.

The voyage to Norway took about three days. Thorlák made good on his orders: He traveled with one assistant – no advisors – and brought with him, grudgingly, one narwhal tusk for the royal court. He carried no other gift than this and his Episcopal blessing.

In Trondheim, his reception by Archbishop Eysteinn was warm and genial. Here were two men of like mind and heart. Eysteinn was so steeped in the rule of the Augustinian Canons that he preferred being known as "Augustinus." He whole-heartedly championed Thorlák's embrace of the spiritual renewal being called for in the church throughout Europe. It pleased him greatly to see a man of firm reputation and discipline assuming the seat of Bishop in Iceland, and Eysteinn pledged his support adamantly.

The Archbishop generally enjoyed the support of Norway's King Magnús V in all he did, and each respected the other's authority. However, the feud between Norway and Iceland exceeded any cordiality between the two. Though it was unlikely Jón had any opportunity to make good on his threats, King Magnús' prejudice was strong enough that his associates bristled at the very idea of an Icelander expecting reception without taking responsibility for Iceland's injustices.

In his audience with the King, Thorlák used quiet logic and perseverance. He acknowledged the inhumanity of these aggressions and agreed they were far out of proportion to what began as a verbal dispute. His gift with dialectical reasoning worked to his advantage as he unflinchingly discussed how the pivotal house fire may have started. Was it an accident? Did tempers flare, leading to mistakes made without considering the scale of their consequences? Just so, the Icelandic priest took leave of his temperance in his devastating retaliation. Thorlák's deft balance between mercy and justice surprised the King, who expected the unyielding Icelandic claim of self-defense. Thorlák faced the truth with disarming honesty. He said that priests must adhere to a higher standard of forbearance and self-control, not vengeance. Thorlák made no excuses but begged for understanding, then brought the discussion back to the business at hand. He was not there to address the dispute between Norway and Iceland, but to receive the King's approval of his appointment as Bishop. The two matters were separate and unrelated.

King Magnús was quite impressed by the fairness and humility of this Bishop-elect. He could not find any reason to let the feud impede the consecration of a fellow man of reason, and so he relented, issuing his decree of royal acceptance. As the customary gifts were exchanged, Magnús received Thorlák's blessing with great joy, and declared that the air between the Nordic nations was cleansed of all acrimony. Peace would thrive between the nations as both men prayed for this cause and for one another. Relations between Iceland and Norway remained cordial for as long as Thorlák held office as Bishop, even as Norway later fell into tumult at the death of King Magnús and the rise of King Sverrir, with the eventual exile of Archbishop Eysteinn. For now, mutual blessing rode on the prevailing winds of the North Sea.

On July 2, 1178, Archbishop Eysteinn consecrated Thorlák the Sixth Bishop of Skálholt in a magnificent ceremony attended by both Bishop Eirík of Stavanger and Bishop Páll of Bergen. In the reception that followed, Thorlák spoke at length with Eirík, who had been a fellow student in the 1150s at St. Victor's. He also took great pleasure in getting to know Bishop Páll, who would go on to be a close friend for the rest of his life. Thorlák stayed in Norway just under a month. He was eager to return home and get to work, as his former habits discouraging travel for leisure were still very much on his heart. As he departed, Bishops Eirík and Páll spoke at length with their Archbishop regarding Iceland's new leader. Eysteinn declared that, of all the bishops he had consecrated, none were fully equal in all the qualities Thorlák possessed. "I cannot tell you how wise his way of life has seemed to me better than by saying that I would choose to have the last day of my life such as I saw every one of his days to be." The other men heartily agreed.

Thorlák found his return ship heavily laden with timber as he prepared for departure. The majority of wood in Iceland originated in Norway and the sailors wished to take advantage of the voyage at hand to transport their goods. Thorlák uneasily warned that the load seemed cumbersome, but he was assured the ship was worthy. He remained skeptical even as he boarded.

The journey home should have found Thorlák greatly relieved. Instead, when he stood on the main deck, taking the wind full face, he felt suddenly very small. He was not this wind's playmate. This was a cold, impersonal wind, whipping at him with taunts and slaps. In the rush of activity to make the consecration journey, he had not given much thought to his clash with Jón. Now, the words of accusation roared in his ears. He knew they were spoken in anger, but he knew they contained truth. He had been nominated by Iceland's most powerful chieftain, who used people for his own advancement and expected favors in return. He saw how Jón's flattery enslaved his sister with such blind devotion that by now she turned Örm against anyone who questioned Jón's integrity, including his Uncle Thorlák. He began to weep for the little girl Ragnheið once was, longing for her father and taking solace in the disingenuous manipulation of a man eleven years her senior. He wept for his powerlessness to protect her and the prospect of working with Jón now that they were both Iceland's top leaders. His oldest doubts taunted him, that he was no more than a puppet of his mother, his mentors, and now, Jón. In the relentless light of the unsetting sun, Thorlák knew he had no way to hide his wretchedness, and found himself unable to pray.

It is not known who witnessed what happened next. Thorlák never spoke of it, but he never doubted it was real. The winds continued building, more so than expected, and the ship was tossed erratically as each wave became more violent. Thorlák's fellow shipmen feared the vessel would capsize. They gathered a team and began heaving timber overboard. Oblivious to the mounting danger, Thorlák felt a strong, soothing presence. A voice seemed to whisper: *I am always with you.* In the frantic activity around him, nobody saw this grown man of forty five years finding comfort with someone not visible. Strength filled his heart. He believed he would not have to carry the burden of Iceland by himself. A loud snapping sound overhead suddenly startled everyone, and as they looked up, a blue-violet aurora hovered over the top of the main mast. A smile spread over Thorlák's face as he recognized what his father used to call the sign of favor every sailor wished for, but few ever received: *Saint Elmo's Fire*! The ship's captain took it to mean they would make it through the gale safely. Thorlák knew it was the ratification of the promise he had just heard in his heart. Perhaps both men were correct.

As quickly as the iridescent flame appeared, it vanished. Likewise, as quickly as Thorlák had been overtaken by despair, a deep peace filled his very soul, and from that moment, nothing troubled him for the remainder of his bishopric.

What puzzled Thorlák most when the storm had passed was how a single, freshly plucked daisy could have ended up at his feet. As he held it and studied it, he gazed out over the horizon and whispered, *"Takk fyrir!"* He held on tightly for the rest of the voyage home.

CHAPTER SIXTEEN

BISHOP OF SKÁLHOLT

On August 9, 1178, Bishop Thorlák disembarked onto Icelandic soil as its Consecrated Shepherd. The duties ahead allowed no leisure time, and the bishop remarked how none could carry out this office conscientiously and still have time to entertain guests at the rate his predecessor had.

The tasks at hand were many. Foremost was ordering the finances of the Diocese, which Thorlák started during his transition period and made good progress with the help of several sound businessmen he appointed specifically to be his fiscal experts.

Thorlák had been candid with Eysteinn about the resistance he faced from Jón and Gizur, who were so intertwined with the church hierarchy that each was an unspoken extension of the other's field of influence. Jón had the title of deacon, and Gizur, priest – though these were more in name than office. They and the other chieftains contributed generously to the Diocese and kept the clergy comfortable. In turn, priests knew that challenging the chieftains would jeopardize their use of privately owned churches and cut off their most reliable source of income. The priests could guarantee support from the people when the chieftains promoted their policies. But above all was the reality that, between disputing clans, cases that could not be settled with arbitration devolved into violent, sometimes fatal, confrontations. Priests, and even bishops, were especially vulnerable if they should find themselves on the wrong side of any chieftain.

In Norway, Thorlák appealed to Eysteinn for advice, citing the Archbishop's earlier pastoral letters to Iceland. He felt pressured by Gizur and the Haukadelir on one side, and Jón and the Oddaverjar on the other – with his sister's concubinage another complication altogether. Thorlák asserted his only allegiance was to Almighty God, refusing to pander to any chieftain or clan. Eysteinn, quite pleased, assured Thorlák his full support. Eysteinn agreed that anyone with a high title, priest or chieftain, has a greater burden to set a higher standard of moral conduct. Those who cannot hold to this standard, he said, would anywhere else face the penalty of excommunication.

This brought Thorlák back to his thinking twelve years prior, when he and Bjarni labored to raise moral standards without any standards codified. Thorlák sought permission now to create and enact a Penitential, and Eysteinn greatly favored the idea, pushing Thorlák to make this a priority.

Eysteinn was nothing short of an idealist. He was zealous about the spirit of the Gregorian Reforms and worked tirelessly to elevate his own country to conform to these principles. Essentially, Pope Gregory VII proposed that the Church, at its very essence, was to be looked at as a separate entity from the mainstream institutions of society. First, priests should see their vocation as a calling from God, not a career move. Second, priests should remain celibate, sacrificing the comforts of marriage and assurance of estates for a more radical pouring out of themselves as the Apostles did in bringing the Gospel message to the people. Third, like Holy Orders, Holy Matrimony should be approached as an equally sacred state in life – meaning that marriages must respect the purity of the sacrament. Extramarital activity and conjugal kinship relations stain the sanctity of matrimony and must be curtailed. Fourth, Church property should be treated as sacred ground, not bought and sold and kept as material assets. Finally, the privileges associated with the Church are likewise to be treated as sacred gifts which cannot be purchased or traded. Doing so would desecrate the very Divinity of the Church as Christ's Body. One could no more buy and sell privileges than they could salvation itself – although there were many who attempted to do both. Pope Gregory VII wanted a definitive end to all of the abuses to the sacred character of the Church.

Eysteinn felt the Gregorian Reforms succinctly summarized a Bishop's duties and suggested they form the basis for the Penitential. Thorlák agreed, mindful also of his thesis on *Decretum Ivo di Chartres*. As in Kirkjubær, Thorlák sought to explain each point in a way that could help penitents know the reason for each rule, rather than hearing them as chastisements or arbitrary regulations. As he used to tell Bjarni, compliance is pointless unless it grows out of mutual love between God and His people.

Armed with a concise agenda, and the backing of his Archbishop, Thorlák felt renewed. He had everything he needed. It was simply a matter of getting to work.

In the main chamber of the Bishop's Estate were
hung the vestments proper to the Bishop's office.
Behind them hung the white robe and black cape
which Thorlák had brought from his belongings at
Thykkvibær. Silently renewing his allegiance to the
Rule of St. Augustine, and pausing for a long
moment in prayer to ask for the spiritual patronage
of the former Bishop of Hippo, Thorlák vested
himself in the everyday garb of a Canon Regular
and set out to begin his tenure in Skálholt.

CHAPTER SEVENTEEN

THE DAILY LIFE OF THORLÁK

Bishop Thorlák seldom rested. His days were filled with ordinary business, and he attended to each matter as diligently as he ever had done in his priestly days. Thorlák felt it was his obligation to see that no need slipped past him, however minor or pressing it might be.

Surrounding his agenda on every side were the canonical hours to which he willingly subjected himself. For, even with the copious obligations of a bishop, he did not cease living the life of a Canon Regular. Each morning he began with Lauds at 3:00, followed by a formula he himself devised. He sang the *Credo* and *Pater Noster* prayers, followed by the hymn *Jesu Nostra Redemptio.* Returning to his dressing chamber in silence, he meditated on what it means to love God and be loved by Him in return. Then, as he dressed, Bishop Thorlák intoned the soaring Gregorian morning hymns of *Nocte Surgentes Vigilemus, Ecce Iam Noctis Tenuatur Umbra* and *Primo Dierum Omnium.* Following that came Psalm One, his favorite, sung in his most robust baritone voice – which few ever heard.

Now dressed for the day, Thorlák went out to the main church where he sang the Litany of the Saints, particularly invoking the prayers of those whose relics were housed in the altars there; and then he read the Office of the Blessed Virgin Mary, meditating silently on her purity, her maternal protection and her powerful intercession for Iceland before God. After this, he prostrated himself before the main altar and remained there in earnest prayer of reparation for the sins of his countrymen. It was here he completed the penances he assigned and then transferred to himself during the Confessions he heard, repeating what he had begun in Kirkjubær. This period of prayer went on for as long as needed, often prolonged by the sheer number of penitents whose burdens he chose to lighten – and the sheer weight of each burden. With the composition and implementation of his Penitential for Iceland, Confessions steadily increased in both frequency and quantity of sins identified and absolved, and Thorlák's voluntary share increased in kind.

As the hour approached 6:00, he rose from the floor and offered Holy Mass for the day, which his countrymen said was more beautiful than any liturgy they had ever seen. Finally, Thorlák set about to his pastoral affairs as most of his colleagues were just awakening. Throughout each day's work he chanted from the psalter and prayers of the Church. As he worked about each day, he easily prayed a third of the psalter, if not more. At bedtime – usually, around midnight – he concluded his repertoire with the hymn *Domine Quis Habitabit*.

Along with sacrificing sleep, Thorlák also fasted from food and drink with remarkable devotion. He downplayed his sacrifice out of genuine concern that people might try to imitate his practices, for he himself acknowledged that he fasted with greater severity than most people could safely tolerate. He did this, he said, hand in hand with administration of his Penitential. The bishop asserted that he could not expect his countrymen to abruptly cease engaging in habits which, though not good for the soul, gave physical comfort in the face of harsh living and hard work. He lived solidarity in sacrifice. He felt it only proper that he give up as much as his people were asked to do, and he did this the only way he could. He also fasted specifically to develop the discipline needed to counteract any temptation he might face toward putting his own comfort before the care of others. Thorlák lived such a virtuous life that there simply was nothing left after food, drink and sleep that he could offer – and so, he offered those, gladly. His fasting was never widely known except among his closest advisors. He lived his sacrifices faithfully, even amidst dinners and banquets at which he was frequently a guest of honor. Never wishing to disappoint his hosts, Thorlák deftly sipped the top of his drink, drawing more air than anything else, and bringing food to his mouth without taking more than a fleeting taste. He gave every appearance of feasting, yet consumed so little that his friends feared for his health. They often brought healers to him with many attempts to boost his flagging stamina, but in the end, nothing worked as would have a full meal and a long night's sleep.

The moments which brought Thorlák pleasure were those spent in the company of his countrymen, just as had been the case many years ago. He sought out people's stories and reflected upon each one with as much personal delight as pastoral interest. He seldom partook in any sort of game but did not begrudge others their pastimes. At home at the Bishop's Estate, he read as many books as he could obtain, and maintained a sizeable library which he actively encouraged the priests of the Diocese to use for their own benefit. He also wrote prolifically in sheepskin volumes. The Diocese of Skálholt was blessed to amass a treasury of homilies, doctrinal treatises, essays and beautifully heartfelt poetry, straight from their own Bishop. When he was not writing, he lost himself thinking… or, in listening to music. Thorlák took great pleasure in string instruments, and it seemed he disappeared altogether when the low-toned compositions of the bowed lyre gave him rich accompaniment when he dared allow his voice to be heard.

As to what kind of leader he was, all agreed that Thorlák was, above all else, a teacher. His love of wisdom came through every word he spoke, and his gift of explaining lofty concepts in plain language made him a joy to listen to. In his Episcopal duties, Thorlák regularly met with priests to instruct them in matters of liturgy, prayer, fasting, contemplating the Gospels and understanding the sacraments. When he taught them, it was almost like a retreat. To the recently ordained, he focused heavily on the first letter of St. Peter, chapter five:

"

God's flock is in your midst; give it a shepherd's care.
Watch over it willingly as God would have you do, not
under constraint nor for shameful profit, but generously.
Be examples to the flock, not lording it over them, so that
when the Chief Shepherd appears, you will win for
yourselves the unfading crown of glory."

Few ever realized how arduous this endeavor was
for Thorlák, each and every time, regardless of how
many times he had previously given the same talk.
Any time he began to speak, he still found his
words might seize in his throat, no less dramatically
than if someone were choking him. It was
physically painful, and horribly humiliating. Each
involuntary, strangulated pause reminded him of his
mother scolding him for "holding his breath," or
the brusque remarks from teachers and schoolmates
mocking him.

Thorlák wondered how he could speak regularly on
such a grand scale. He devoted a morning to this in
prayer prostrated before the altar. There, he
imagined what his voice might look like. To him, it
was an injured bird, still able to fly but thrashing
about in not fully succeeding. He imagined lifting
this bird up to the Heavenly Throne and offering it
as Mary and Joseph had offered turtle doves, the

offering of the poor, when they presented Jesus in the Temple. He prayed, "Father, I offer Thee my voice, poor and broken, as all that I have with which to praise You." In his mind, he saw the Hand of God take up this bird and tenderly kiss it, whispering in gentle reply, "*I love you.*" As Thorlák meditated further, he imagined the bird lifting its head toward the Father's kiss, uttering forth a surprisingly joyful song. He envisioned the bird flying crookedly back to his hands, taking it to his own breast and saying, "I love you, too." From that day on, Thorlák struggled as often as he ever had with his speech, but each episode reminded him that his poorly spoken words were loved even in their brokenness, and he saw no need to despise something that God Himself did not.

The two most common words people used when talking about Bishop Thorlák were "mild" and "gentle." He brought smiles to the faces of everyone who saw him approaching, and he brought an authentic holiness to the land like none had previously known.

It was an ordinary day, one year into his consecrated bishopric, when the Diocese of Skálholt received in official salutation a pastoral

letter written by His Excellency, Archbishop
Eysteinn of Niðaros. As Thorlák read the contents,
he braced his jaw and shoulders, which Icelanders
often do reflexively when the ground begins to
tremble. Southerners know earthquakes well, living
as neighbors to the ill-tempered volcanic giants
Hekla, Katla and Eyjafjallajökull. The sons of
Iceland mimic their geological counterparts in
temperament. As natives know, when opposing
tectonic plates – or tempers – clash, the scalding
heat which escapes can do more damage than flying
debris.

Thorlák inhaled deeply… and, re-reading the last
line, knew that it was Eysteinn's personal nod of
encouragement, cloaked in a familiar quotation of
St. Augustine:

> *"God provides the wind, but man must raise the sails.
> The time to rise is now."*

Iceland's moral sails were about to be hoisted for
what would go on to define the remainder of
Thorlák's episcopacy.

CHAPTER EIGHTEEN

EYSTEINN'S LETTER

Bishop Thorlák held the pastoral letter while Jón and Gizur sat and wondered what awaited them. Neither could imagine why Thorlák had summoned them both to this meeting behind closed doors.

"My brothers in Christ," Thorlák began at last, "the entire people of Iceland hold you both in highest esteem. Archbishop Eysteinn concurs – you are indeed men of high status."

The two looked at one another. Was there to be an appointment, a conferral of some new title within the Church?

Thorlák continued. "As you know, I have worked diligently to complete and codify our new Penitential for the spiritual benefit of the Icelandic people."

Gizur interjected, "You mean, the Book of Subjection of the Icelandic people to Gratian Rule? Our existing laws, *Kristinréttur hinn forni*, are more than sufficient for the Church in Iceland. The Gratian Rule is excessive to the point of absurdity, in its dictation of private matters of conduct."

"No," Thorlák corrected. "The Penitential draws more from *Decretum Ivo di Chartres* than *Decretum Gratiani*. It is rooted in the theology of human relationships."

"Hugh of St. Victor," Jón added, sardonically. "Thorlák lives and breathes by Hugh of St. Victor."

"Regardless," Thorlák said, focusing once more on the letter at hand, "I need to know how familiar you are with the new Icelandic Penitential."

"We know it well," said Jón. Gizur nodded in agreement.

"Good," said Thorlák. "Then, if you please, would you recite for me the statutes on Holy Matrimony, particularly regarding marital fidelity?"

The men appeared confused. "What does this have to do with His Excellency's appointments?" asked Gizur.

"This is not a decree of conferral. This letter is a stern warning to me, stating if I do not review with you the standards of conduct expected of married men, I will be in violation of my Office as Bishop — that is to say, I am being ordered to execute the prescribed penalties within the Penitential for those who disregard the standards of moral conduct, irrespective of social standing or title."

Jón and Gizur were at a loss to understand. After a long pause, Thorlák said, plainly, "It means, if you continue flagrantly disregarding your marital covenants, you will each be excommunicated."

The two men gasped indignantly. Thorlák continued, "This is a matter of grave concern. His Excellency has singled you each out by name." Thorlák added, "I am prepared to address this with you, here, today, individually, before it comes to such drastic measures. Let us take on this task now, once and for all, so that our Diocese can be an example of right order from the top down and we may disregard this pastoral warning."

Jón, enraged, shouted in defiance. "No man's laws dictate the personal matters of any other man! It is between myself and my God, and none other! Not you, not Gratian, not Eysteinn! None!"

Gizur mused in silent anger. Thorlák sat, calmly, looking upon his two advisors without a word.

"You will not excommunicate me!" Jón exclaimed. "The very threat of excommunication is a threat to your own life!"

Thorlák remained silent.

Jón swore to himself in seething anger several more times before approaching the Bishop with both fists clenched. "You will not excommunicate me! I am the grandson of a king! If I do not kill you first, I assure you, my kinsfolk will do so before I can!"

Thorlák extended his right hand. "May the Lord God Almighty have mercy on you, Jón, and wash away your iniquity…"

The words which Jón uttered against his Bishop cannot be repeated for their offensiveness and sheer hatred. As when facing down one of Skálholt's easterly squalls, Thorlák fixed his face and took the lacerating wind of Jón's fury full force.

Gizur, still reticent, sat engrossed in thought of his own. Jón left, promising that this matter would be dismissed by the time he returned. Thorlák inquired, softly, "Are you ready, Gizur, to have your Confession heard?"

Gizur Hallsson met the eyes of his bishop and, for the first time in his life, felt small.

"Come," Thorlák said. "We can do this together. I will lead the way."

Gizur rose and followed, surprisingly unafraid.

CHAPTER NINETEEN

EPISODES OF THE EPISCOPATE

The problems of Gizur Hallsson were not solved immediately upon confessing them to Bishop Thorlák, who willingly extended the process over several weeks in an extraordinary act of pastoral instruction. Thorlák heard Gizur's confessions using the Penitential as a guide, taking meticulous care with each question to thoroughly explain the theology, moral law and Canon Law behind its codification. As with his other penitents, Thorlák assigned Gizur's penances by the book, and then reduced them significantly by taking on the greater part of their burden himself. Gizur was a reluctant student, arguing copious points with his confessor yet finding, in the end, little ground between admitting his violations and having Thorlák take the penalties for him. It was not a disciplinary problem, but rather, the examination of character which disarmed the chieftain the most.

Gizur's bigger challenge was amending his ways privately within a very public political life. He could not simply walk away from his family, the Haukadelir clan, and the influence they held throughout Iceland. His mistresses were unwilling to sever their relationships because their association with him elevated their own status and that of their illegitimate children. Bishop Thorlák worked on a plan for Gizur to support all who depended on his livelihood while practicing continence – in other words, celibacy – in these relationships, to be a better moral example to those in his path. The stubborn chieftain railed indignantly against voluntary abstinence, claiming that it was impossible, unnatural and unnecessary to deny the attraction between men and women. Gizur accused Thorlák of being pigheaded about pleasures he had himself never tasted, and therefore, had no right to regulate. On the contrary, Thorlák asserted that he was very well aware that the conjugal relationship was the greatest enjoyment of this world, but that its purpose far surpassed the degradation it received when turned into a transaction for gratification.

Gizur may have been correct that Thorlák had never experienced the consummation between man and woman, but he underestimated Thorlák's appreciation of the depths of love and the longings of the human heart. Thorlák was very well schooled in the rich Victorine dissertations on St.

Augustine's cry, "*My heart is restless until it rests in You, my God!*" Many overlooked the fact that Thorlák had always been closely attuned to the emotions of the people surrounding him. On any Icelandic farmstead, turf dwellings were constructed with heat retention in mind, not privacy. Every Icelander grew up with a matter-of-fact knowledge that men and women came together to conceive children because this took place routinely in the common rooms where everyone openly slept along the perimeter. Love was the one thing at the end of the day that soothed the muscles, kindled joy and reminded adults why, when morning arrived, it was worth going out and laboring all over again. Thorlák did not flinch from love or disapprove of its expression. Quite the opposite, he marveled at the miracle of love's creative and sustaining power. A good majority of his essays and homilies dealt with love and the connection between God and human relationships. Thorlák was no prude. But, as with everything else, he saw both a lower order and a higher order. Those who followed after God would find the higher order and experience love more abundantly, while those who exploited affection for their own gratification would glean little nourishment.

Gizur Hallsson was not immediately converted by Thorlák's teachings, but he did make a gradual effort to curtail his extramarital behavior.

Meanwhile, Jón Loftsson continued, flagrantly as ever, with his life as before the pastoral admonition. His mistresses reveled in his attention. His children, legitimate and illegitimate, were all raised in comfort and grooming for political lives. By now, Páll was a polished statesman and Örm was in training for the priesthood at Oddi. As conscientiously as Thorlák tried to be present to his nephews, only Páll responded regularly. Örm seemed threatened by his uncle, leaving him baffled. He suspected, correctly, that Jón swayed Örm's opinion that the bishop was a headstrong adherent to literal theology that was not practical outside academia.

Thorlák was active in all aspects of Church administration. Although he delegated financial matters to those specifically retained for those duties, he took close interest in regulating the day to day operations of the Church according to Canon Law. He formed his approach around Augustine's *Rex Iustus*, the notion that God is the central authority, and that all earthly rulers, including

Icelandic chieftains, were merely God's regents, not authorities unto themselves.

With family church ownership already a sticking point for many in the Diocese, Bishop Thorlák worked tirelessly to teach people that the only true change would be in their minds and hearts – to step back and realize that their labor and materials may have erected these structures, but the result is something to be given over – *consecrated* – to God, for God's use. Those who built the church would remain its caretakers. He successfully convinced many that he was not seizing rights from landowners so much as he sought to consecrate the land to God under their stewardship.

Most were willing to accept this. The chieftains, however, openly opposed this policy, demanding the disputes be publicly mediated in the forum of the *Althing*. Those who challenged Thorlák had many rulings go their way, courtesy of political favors granted by Jón Loftsson and his connections.

Heavily encouraged by Archbishop Eysteinn, Thorlák faced the reality that people openly defying Church rules voluntarily removed themselves from the communion of the faithful. He knew that a father is sometimes called upon to teach hard lessons to his children, and that a Bishop likewise has to enforce the rules of the Church in order to shepherd the faithful. Thus, Thorlák became the first Icelandic bishop ever to invoke excommunication upon those who flaunted noncompliance with Church regulations.

Excommunication was notoriously known by grim rumors of bell, book and candle. With Iceland such a small and interdependent nation, ostracization was more than just a social construct: it was a matter of life and death. In a society tight-knit by necessity, one excommunicated would not only lose the ability to receive the sacraments, but the very ties on which they depend daily.

In reality, none could truly be banished in Iceland without leaving the island or the district in which they lived. The excommunicated would cease to attend Mass and social functions within their family, but few were ever truly shunned. Excommunication was a severe spiritual consequence with few practical ramifications. This was of little concern to the bishop, who knew that the loss of sacramental participation jeopardized the soul, which was far greater peril than losing one's connections in the community. Thorlák would go to every length possible to avoid this end.

As a result, Bishop Thorlák, the reluctant speaker, became adept at pleading cases in public. When it came to battling for souls, Thorlák found his words flowed abundantly, and he never hesitated to passionately lecture unrepentant sinners in a fervent attempt to keep them in the flock.

Many listened. Some did not, and were declared excommunicated. For every individual he excommunicated, Thorlák wept.

Of all those who complied with these property reforms, Jón Loftsson remained steadfastly disobedient.

It happened on Jón's estate of Höfðabrekka that a storm heavily damaged his church building. It was meticulously restored over the course of several months, and at its completion, Jón called an assembly to celebrate its rededication. Bishop Thorlák arrived as expected, and requested the deed from Jón to begin the consecration.

Jón gleefully refused.

Unleashing a torrent of mockery, Jón Loftsson made a show of defiance by surrounding Thorlák with a battalion of axe-wielding allies proclaiming the church property of the Oddaverjar. Jón accused the bishop of extortion and abuse of power, enumerating every church building acquired by the Diocese and inciting onlookers to indignation over the notion that Thorlák used his education to trick unsuspecting common folk into surrendering their hard-earned income. Thorlák stood quietly. He looked from side to side, seeing the weapons raised against him, and, leveling his eyes at Jón, spoke only these words: "Deliver me from my enemies, O my God, and defend me from them that rise up against me." With that, Thorlák left, making no effort to challenge his foes. Jón declared victory, and a cheer arose in the crowd. Before the bishop could get too far, Jón shouted a warning: "Take note, Your Excellency, that your days of tyranny are numbered!"

It was true that from that day forward, property owners were not as willing to comply with Thorlák's decree on church ownership. The Oddaverjar dominated that region. Some felt safe defying the bishop knowing they had Jón Loftsson's backing. Others were afraid of being identified as a supporter of Thorlák. Jón's actions did not result in his excommunication that day, but they badly eroded Thorlák's relationship with the people he so wanted to shepherd.

Overall, Bishop Thorlák had moderate success aligning private churches with proper ownership. He put an end to the practice of laymen naming their own priests to the churches they built on their land. In the course of fifteen years, he oversaw the consecration of twenty three churches, ten of which he specially named in honor of the Blessed Virgin Mary as thanksgiving for her presence with him through the arduous and thankless tasks of accounting for these properties.

There were numerous other acts which strengthened the spiritual integrity of the faith in Iceland and brought it into closer alignment with the Catholic Church worldwide. The liturgical calendar was amended to include the feasts of St. Ambrose (St. Augustine's teacher and mentor) along with St. Cecilia and St. Agnes, and added vigils for the feasts of all twelve apostles and St. Nicholas. The celebration of Pentecost was pushed to the length of an octave and clearer guidelines were given for when and how the faithful should fast at prescribed times throughout the liturgical year. Thorlák instituted a systematic program for priestly formation identifying prerequisites which made it easier on the one hand to know a man's readiness for ordination, but gave him great angst on the other when he was faced with men who fell far short of the standards he codified. Never one to turn anyone away, Thorlák took such postulants under his tutelage until he felt they had reached a level of readiness to proceed. Under the bishop's leadership, the office of priesthood took on a greater integrity and was held with higher respect than ever before.

Of the years Thorlák held the See of Skálholt, the first six were the most ambitious, and the most prosperous. With the backing and praise of Archbishop Eysteinn, Thorlák's bishopric was a model for the rest of Europe in every aspect. The six-year pattern emerged again, however; this time, in an ill-fated turn of events. Sverrir Sigurdsson, a priest in Norway and political rebel discontented with church law, succeeded in ousting both King Magnús and Archbishop Eysteinn from their seats of power and into English exile. The new hostility against Church authority in Norway created a prevailing wind which impeded any further clerical reforms in Iceland… and, which Jón Loftsson found quite favorable.

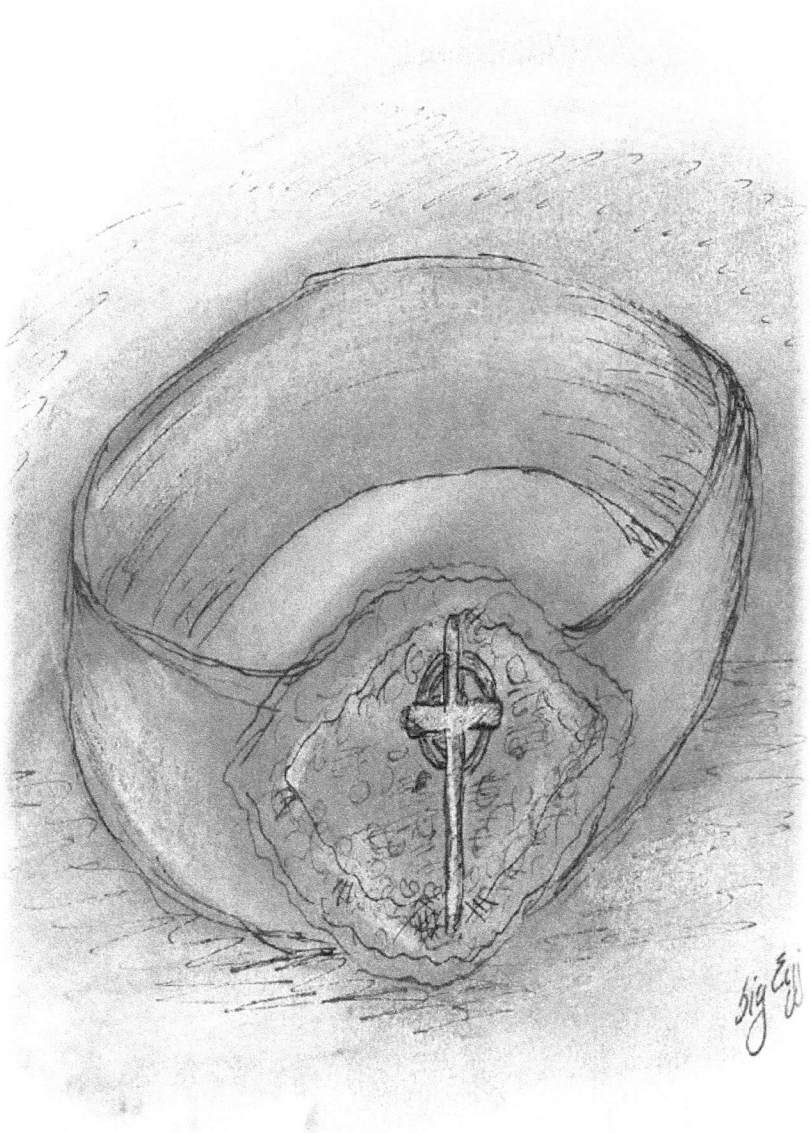

CHAPTER TWENTY

A CONVERSATION WITH PÁLL

It was a placid afternoon in Skálholt when 30-year-old chieftain and deacon Páll Jónsson sat with his uncle in the Bishop's residence. Páll noticed Thorlák's sallow cheeks, and it was clear he was suffering with some internal discomfort, if not outright pain. Nonetheless, Thorlák was genuinely pleased to spend time with his nephew, and was grateful to be obligated to rest for a bit.

"*Frændi*," Páll said. "My father says it is a fraud for the Church to claim property in the name of God. I have studied the same works as you, yet I am stymied by their contradictions. Surely, you must agree it is unjust to seize a man's rightful and hard-earned property for the cause of amassing greater wealth, and therefore, greater power? This contradicts the very tenets of Christianity!"

"You cannot serve both God and Mammon," replied Thorlák. "In his riches, man lacks wisdom."

"Then you say, Uncle, that the Church lacks wisdom when these riches are transferred to her hands?"

"*Sonur minn*," Thorlák said. "Look here." He extended his arm and hand, and let the ring of his consecration catch the afternoon sun. "Why do I wear this bit of metal and stone?"

Páll laughed. "Metal? Is this what you call gold?"

"Gold is a metal," Thorlák answered. "Why gold?"

"The prestige of your office, of course!" exclaimed Páll, laughing again. "You are the highest in the land! You are Episcopal Royalty!"

"Why not a simple band of bog iron, which more greatly reflects my origin?"

"*Frændi!* You speak in riddles! The gold ring sets you apart in high distinction. The greater valued metals go to the greater valued men, and the gemstones add to your collateral."

"Ah," said Thorlák. "Collateral value. Páll: I have just ordered fine woven vestments from the continent for all of our priests in Skálholt. Is this not an extravagance, when they could just as easily wear homespun garments? Is not a priest a man, or his garment?"

"The man who wears seemly attire must act accordingly," Páll mused. "One must live up to his vestments."

Thorlák continued in his train of thought. "And, what of our beeswax candles? Why such excess, when our own oil lamps are most sufficient? Why beeswax candles for Mass?"

"It is elevation toward greater dignity!" Páll answered, perturbed. "The rare and expensive items are as first fruits unto the Lord! Did not God Himself look unfavorably upon Cain's second best when Abel put forth his finest offering?"

Thorlák challenged Páll. "What does that have to do with this day, here, and now? Abel did not import his offering! Must we make such an extravagant show?"

Páll retorted, "God does not measure the worth of material things, only men do!"

Thorlák asked, "So, why have finery at all?"

"Because finery is a statement of high worth, one that sets the valued property apart. Something of high value is cared for more diligently, with greater reverence, with more forethought, with greater investment." Páll seemed satisfied with his response.

"Then," Thorlák said, "Why would we not do the same for the source and summit of our life in the Church? A chapel built on a farmstead for the farmsteaders is a farmstead chapel. A church erected for the glory of God is to be set apart, cared for more diligently, with greater investment."

Páll stared at Thorlák's consecration ring. "And you… this ring…?"

Thorlák looked at Páll directly. "This ring reminds me every day of the investment the Church has made in me, to be God's vicar and shepherd of His people; and, of my obligation to live up to that investment. This ring does not change my character. I am the same man now as I was before the ring was given to me. But it obligates me to behave as a man worthy of gold… not bog iron, which I more truly deserve."

Páll was silent.

Thorlák continued. "I have tried to show your father this principle, but he is convinced that a man's value consists in his worth to others. He can never experience the greatness of God's love because he feels only as loved as he is useful. Unfortunately, many people do find him useful, which has taken away any need he has for God or God's love."

Páll listened intently as Thorlák added, "I have also tried to give your brother a greater sense of the dignity of his office as a priest by allocating him the Breiðabolstaður estate. I fear the message is lost in the shadow of ambition."

Thorlák was correct. Örm, now ordained, joined Jón in mocking Thorlák's magnanimous entrustment of this prestigious Church-held estate to his nephew, accusing the Bishop of nepotism and calling him a hypocrite – but taking hold of the property nonetheless.

Páll spoke quietly. "My father hates everything about you," he said. "But I don't know why."

"Your father is starving spiritually," Thorlák said. "I remember when he was a student at Oddi. He had a lot of pressure on him from the very beginning. His kinsfolk gave him the burden of royalty before he ever had a choice."

Páll raised his head. "But – is not that what we just discussed, that we are to rise up to value expected of us?"

Thorlák corrected him, gently and sadly. "No. This is the inverse. We are all men of bog iron. We know this, deep in our hearts. God lifts us up to His bosom anyway, dressing us in finery because He, the Great King, loves us. It is that love to which we must live up. No, Jón has been wrongly told that he is a man of gold, and he has spent his entire life building defenses around something he cannot be of his own accord. To prove his worth, he must never show his need. And… to never be needy is to never be fully known, or fully loved, for who we truly are. It is to deny ourselves our very humanity."

Thorlák's voice cracked and he stopped speaking. Páll noticed his moist eyelids but said nothing. After a moment's pause, Páll stood, preparing to leave. He turned back and gave his uncle a tight embrace. Then, he departed.

CHAPTER TWENTY ONE

THORLÁK CONFRONTS JÓN

Thorlák systematically accomplished everything he set out to do at the time of his consecration. The Diocese was on solid fiscal ground. He defined the standards by which the priests and chieftains were to abide, and clearly delineated what a Christian life looked like in all walks of life. Most importantly, he exemplified each of these areas himself, in the way he lived and conducted himself as Bishop.

Thorlák's achievements at the Diocesan level were a remarkable show of sound management. He proved himself a strong leader and a wise diplomat. When he was called upon to arbitrate disputes, his deft employment of dialectical logic left few people dissatisfied, including those who lost their claims. But on a personal level, Thorlák was the same man about the Bishop's Estate as he had been in any of his parishes. It was not as easy for him to mingle about without drawing attention to himself, and so he took to inviting groups of common folk to his residence for dinner. When he did so, he preceded the meal by a welcoming ceremony in which he bestowed each guest with a gift, and concluded by washing the feet of each visitor. It became his custom to seek out those who had few relatives or appeared lonely, but his invitation to them was startling in its sincerity. In so many words, Bishop Thorlák asked these people if they would be his friends, not the other way around – soliciting in his genuine need for their companionship, not from plenty or out of pity. He honestly, desperately wanted friendship with people he could be with as himself, without pomp or office or performance.

One man in particular who had terrible, chronic infections became such a dear friend that Thorlák gave him residence at the Bishop's Estate in his dying months for the sake of caring for him and gleaning the most time with him before he succumbed to his illness. Thorlák's advisors questioned him, wondering who this man was to him and praising his charity. Thorlák's correction was sincere: "He is here in much greater measure to serve me," he said. "I draw strength from his lack of pretense."

The one area of his episcopate in which Thorlák was not yet satisfied was in how he might better address the institution of Holy Matrimony. Although he approached the topic individually in

Confession and preached on marital fidelity in his public homilies, the elevation of marriage to the height of a sacrament remained an elusive target. The opposition seemed steeper in Iceland than elsewhere. Alliances between families and accumulation of property were held as tantamount to the survival of the nation. Devastating seasons and high mortality rates tore families apart routinely, and the matter of consanguinity was difficult to speak to among a population of few more than 70,000 people in any given year. Yet, armed with his Penitential and recalling the Victorine treatises on love, he set out to champion Holy Matrimony as both embodiment and source of God's life-giving grace.

Thorlák may never have played games with his peers, but he was unquestionably a master strategist. Following the same thinking as when he ministered at Kirkjubær, Thorlák seeded his ideas among the people from the bottom up. He used his Penitential as a teaching tool to instruct penitents about the design of marriage, but then he devised a clever modification to the prescriptions for violations of marital fidelity. Penalties for sins were usually assigned in quantities of prayer or by monetary fine.

Confessors could easily raise funds for their parishes by collecting fines from penitents, and many disgruntled parishioners complained at the exploitation of their transgressions for Church gain. Thorlák, too, levied fines in his penances; however, he did so with deliberate design. Sins against marriage were fined according to degree of severity, and the money collected went directly to families who were in dire need. Thorlák thus established a fund for families who observed their marital covenant in spite of temptation and adversity, supplied and replenished by fines collected from those who abused their marital vows. He made this practice well known and clearly explained so that penances took on meaning to those who paid them, and those who endured the hardships of married life were rewarded for their fidelity. This practice quelled many complaints while reinforcing canonical teaching – and fortified many families who might have otherwise broken apart, as Thorlák's own had so many years before.

The people slowly, steadily saw that Church laws regarding marriage were neither arbitrary nor unjust. Icelanders accepted reform as cautiously as the vegetation trying to colonize the lava fields, but the effect was noticeable. The proof was found not so much in the parishes of the poor, but in the outcry from the elite – who saw this shift as a direct threat to their comfort and power.

Thorlák's quiet campaign to sanctify the Sacrament of Matrimony exploded at the top level when public officials refused to comply with the regulations that had always been in place but never before enforced. One by one, Thorlák brought cases of illicit relationships to the fore and decisively dissolved their unions. Irregular marriage contracts of prominent priests and chieftains were called to account with equal fervor, the violations enumerated aloud and the relationships declared null and void. This was no easy task, and drew quite a bit of public attention each time another case was heard. The most notorious involved a prominent priest who betrothed his daughter to a man known to be a cousin, flagrantly overlooking the laws against consanguinity. Each was involved in other relationships that negated the purity of their intentions, if indeed Holy Matrimony was their desired end. Thorlák plainly declared this couple's intended union no more than strategic family posturing and declared the entire prospect a ruse and an insult to the integrity of the sacrament. The betrothal was decisively broken by Thorlák, who added that all involved would be excommunicated if they persisted in their obstinacy.

Among those supporting this priest and his daughter was Jón Loftsson. Jón took every opportunity he could to publicly resist Bishop Thorlák, and was rumored to have conspired on several occasions to ambush the bishop and take him captive. Each time, his plans fell short, for one reason or another. One day, as Thorlák was dining at the house of one of the prominent Þingmenn, word came through that Jón prepared one of his sons to assassinate the bishop on his way to Vespers. As the matter was discussed, Thorlák's friends begged him not to leave, their fear increasing by the moment. Thorlák calmly assured them that all would be well. When he rose to leave, he ordered his companions to stay behind for their safety. Their protests did nothing to dissuade Thorlák, who made his way outdoors and toward the chapel as planned. From the shadows came a figure, which Thorlák made out to be a man wielding an axe. He stopped. The man advanced, raising the axe over his head. Thorlák looked him in the eye, and, inexplicably, the man became paralyzed in this threatening position. Breaking his gaze, but saying nothing, Thorlák continued on and entered the chapel, unharmed.

Thorlák was pained greatly by the acrimony sown by this rivalry. As much as he desired redemption for Jón, he could not deny the personal repulsion he held toward him, and begged God to somehow allow healing to take place. Thorlák knew the day would come when he must take Jón into account for his actions, his defiance, and his violations of his marital covenant, and, frankly, he wished to avoid that day for as long as possible.

Before he made any plan to act, Thorlák called Ragnheið to his residence and attempted to reason with her. With her sons fully grown and holding prestigious chieftaincies, Ragnheið felt no need to yield to any of Thorlák's pleadings to end her relationship with Jón. She dismissed his logic as folly, insulting him for keeping dull and uncompromising allegiance to ridiculous ideals. In an unusual turn, Thorlák interrupted his sister with the impassioned anger of a man in pain.

"You are a child of god, Ragnheið!"

"God loves you!"

Just as uncharacteristically, Ragnheið stopped shouting... and listened.

"I have watched you waste your entire life waiting to be loved by someone who will never love you! When will you look up and realize you do not need a man's empty flattery – because you are already loved?"

Ragnheið's face burned. For once, she had no words of retaliation.

Thorlák embraced his sister for the first time he could ever remember. As he did, he whispered, "Our Pabbi loved you." She raised her head and said, "But he was weak."

"He loved," replied Thorlák. "He was not weak. He loved. A man who loves, does so because he knows his strength is not in himself, but in the Lord, who is Love. A man who finds strength in himself cannot love."

Ragnheið remained silent. Then, she said, "No matter. It is too late, now." Thorlák corrected her.

"It is never late in eternity. It is always now. God is ready to receive you whenever you are ready to need Him."

"Then," she said after several moments, "let my life begin."

The never-married sister of Bishop Thorlák, now past her fiftieth birthday, would find that opportunity before the end of the year.

****

Thorlák surveyed the azure summer sky crowning the Skálholt cathedral and imagined what a new steeple might look like. Thorlák recalled the magnificent peal of the bells in Lincoln and wondered if such majesty could be replicated across Iceland's southern plains. He mused that, without cobblestone streets and castle walls, the wind might just snatch the toll away before it could be caught and reverberated by the mountainside.

His reverie did not last long. The tension in the gathering crowd was mounting, and Thorlák needed to focus on the task at hand. Of all the times he had previously confronted Jón Loftsson, this was the one instance he felt unsteady on his feet. The pain below his breastbone seemed pronounced this day and he made an unusual appeal in his prayers for relief.

The shouts of the onlookers announced Jón's approach, and the bishop steeled himself. His mouth should not feel this dry.

"Let us get on with the proceedings, shall we, Your Excellency?" Jón's confident greeting was far from cordial.

"As you wish." Thorlák cleared his throat. "Jón Loftsson: As witnessed by God and Church, you entered willingly into the covenant of Holy Matrimony with Halldora Brandsdottir. Is this true?"

"It is."

"You stand accused today of infidelity to your marital covenant. How do you answer this charge?"

"It is true."

"Then, by the authority of the Catholic Church, I command you to renounce here all relationships into which you have entered illicitly, or face the consequence of excommunication."

Jón smiled, calculatingly. "Call down excommunication as you will… for, I will not allow you or any other man to dictate whom I should love."

"Love?" Thorlák felt his composure waver. "Is that how you justify exploiting the affections of four women while your wife languishes at home?"

"I have exploited no woman," Jón replied. "The love of which I speak is both genuine and reciprocal." He added, slyly, "Ragnheið will tell you so."

"Ragnheið was a child!" Thorlák retorted. "She looked to you as a mentor, not a lover!"

"Ragnheið LOVES ME!" Jón shouted, visibly shaking. "SHE IS THE ONLY ONE WHO EVER HAS!"

"That is where you are wrong," Thorlák said. "God loved you first. He always has. And He still does. This is your day to experience God's love, in making your shrift."

"I WILL NOT!" spat Jón. Regaining his breath, he said, "I will not deny what is true! I love Ragnheið! I always have, and I always will, to my dying day!"

"If you love her," Thorlák said, "then you must desire what is best for her, not consign her to a life of iniquity. If it is Ragnheið you love… send her away. Keeping her as your concubine affirms your interests above all else."

Jón gasped, and asserted: "I will part from Ragnheið only when God Himself breathes it in my breast to do so!" With that, he summoned his entourage, and made to depart.

Thorlák was a bit surprised at how quickly the encounter ended. His advisors gathered about him. Gizur Hallsson spoke first: "Your Excellency, you are left with no choice but excommunication." Murmurs went about the group, and then a voice cried out, "I beg of you! Do not exact this sentence until I have made one more appeal, of my own pleading!"

The supplicant approached Thorlák and took both of the bishop's hands into his own. "You have shown forbearance this long; surely, you can allow one more attempt at reconciliation, which I myself will make."

Thorlák met the chieftain's eyes to see the boy he had blessed on the black sand shore three decades prior, and could not speak. Grimly, he nodded his consent.

"May God's mercy go before me," Páll said, and squeezed his uncle's gaunt hands.

"Yes," whispered Thorlák. "Do not delay."

****

"Faðir!" Páll caught up with Jón, having the advantage of riding horseback while Jón headed on foot to the farmstead of one of his allies. He quickly dismounted.

"What is it, Páll?"

"I have a favor to ask."

Jón stepped away from the group, waving them onward so that he could speak to his son alone. "If it is the matter of disposing of this bishop, I swear, I will accomplish this myself if need be!"

"My mother," Páll began, "is a worthy woman."

Jón looked confused.

"My mother is a woman who has given me everything I have ever needed. She has devoted her entire life to my wellbeing and that of my brother.

And yet," Páll said, "she accomplished this without having the benefit of marriage."

Jón stared in disbelief as Páll continued. "My mother is a worthy woman. She may be past the age of childbearing, but she is admirable in her skill and stamina. She is resourceful, dedicated, and —" Páll hesitated. "And, she is a woman who loves with her very self, even to the point of giving up her rights to marriage, to fulfill the love which she first promised in her youth and has carried out faithfully ever since."

Jón's face was like stone. "I would like to ask," Páll said, "that you reward my mother's devotion by giving her at last the dignity she deserves."

Before his father could speak, Páll added, "As the great-grandson of a king, do you not agree that my lineage should be honorable?"

"Your mother," Jón said, far away in his thoughts, "is the fairest woman in all of Iceland." He looked up, off to the horizon. "That was never flattery. I mean that, most sincerely."

"Then, I pray: Do not let her die alone. Do not let her die in iniquity."

Jón studied Páll for a long time. "It is hard to deny," he said at last, "that you bear the blood of that Bishop in your princely veins."

"As does the woman you love," Páll said. "Which may be the very reason she loves you as she does."

CHAPTER TWENTY TWO

THE DECLINE OF BISHOP THORLÁK

When days in Iceland give way to twilight, then nighttime, the peak of the active season has passed. Clement weather continues a bit longer, but the return of the stars and emerald-hued ribbons above is Iceland's signal to finish things undone before the forced rest of winter's unremitting agenda.

Thorlák was six months into his sixtieth year and giving serious thought to retirement. He felt he accomplished all he could and longed to retreat to the quiet enclosure of prayer at Thykkvibær. He examined his years in the Bishop's seat carefully, repeatedly, and concluded that everything he hoped to establish was either in place or in the process of taking root. He did not have the energy to attempt anything more, and he realized that his reforms now depended on the fidelity of those around him, and after him to the next generation.

Jón Loftsson remained a sworn rival but now kept a wide distance from the bishop. After Páll's unexpected act of mediation, Jón made his Confession to a priest friend of his – not Bishop Thorlák – and received full absolution. Through one of many lucrative connections, Jón learned of a farmsteader in Hólar whose wife had died several years prior and arranged a marriage for Ragnheið. It is not known what was said between them as it happened, but those close to Jón knew not to mention the matter for the pain it gave him. Word rarely traveled southward from Hólar, but by Páll's accounts, his mother lived comfortably in her final years.

Thorlák broached his retirement with Gizur, who saw much merit in the idea. The bishop's steadfast adherence to his daily rituals kept him from seeing how rapidly his health was declining. Those in his employ noticed his thin frame, the grimace of his pain, and his growing frailty of step. Thorlák carried on without complaint and completing his journeys throughout the districts of his Diocese before the weather would become prohibitive. He had just returned from one such venture. Gizur reflected on Thorlák's lifetime duty to Church and country, and felt retirement seemed wise.

Thorlák took the next several days to sit and draw up his resignation, carefully considering how to begin the process of transition with those up and coming in Skálholt. He also drafted a petition to be received as a Canon in residence at Thykkvibær.

He rose from his desk to retrieve something he needed, and found his strength suddenly gone. Falling to the floor, he was too weak to rise on his own. He was aware of the commotion this caused, but somehow detached, as if dreaming. He was helped to his feet and carried, one man under each arm, to his bed chamber. He was offered water but could not recall if he drank. Cloudy sleep overtook him and the voices surrounding him faded into silence.

Some time later, Bishop Thorlák awakened. He was alert but could not quite catch his breath. His mouth was dry and his hands cold. As he tried to sit up in bed, he did not know how to summon the strength to do so.

"He is awake!" shouted one of his advisors. Gizur Hallsson appeared in the doorway.

"Your Excellency!" Gizur exclaimed. "We are here with you. The healers have examined you, and the priests at Thykkvibær have asked to come and anoint you."

"What do the healers say?" asked Thorlák, barely audible.

Gizur knelt beside his bishop. "It is not curable," he said. "The signs are very grim."

As though to punctuate Gizur's pronouncement, Thorlák experienced a sharp, stabbing pain under his ribs. He held his breath and winced until it subsided, and understood without question that he was not going to recover.

"Thykkvibær…" he said, with a sorrowful tone. "I make you come to me instead."

Thorlák closed his eyes again. Silently, Gizur wiped the tears from his own face.

"I pray I have paid back my benefactors by the life I have lived," Thorlák said from his bolster.

Gizur, speaking firmly, said, "You have lived a life of such virtuous example that none will ever equal your sanctity!"

Thorlák's eyes remained closed. After a moment longer, Gizur left, knowing there were many tasks of dire importance that needed administration at once. Almost immediately, Thorlák slept.

CHAPTER TWENTY THREE

BISHOP THORLÁK'S ACT OF MERCY

Whether he heard these words in a dream or by his priest-advisors reading from the Divine Office, a phrase disrupted Thorlák's mind and caused him great distress. It came from the Letter of Saint James, chapter two, verse thirteen:

> *"Judgment without mercy will be shown to any who is not merciful. Mercy triumphs over judgment."*

Thorlák bolted upright. "I must not deprive anyone of the sacraments!"

The two priests keeping watch over Thorlák were quite startled, mostly at the surge of strength from their gravely ill bishop, and then at the confusing nature of his words. He looked imploringly to them and begged, "Please, do not delay! The sacraments are fundamental to the restoring mankind to the knowledge of God's mercy! To deprive my countrymen of what God has sent through His Son is complicity in the starvation of their souls!"

Thorlák had such alarm in his eyes that his fellow priests thought he might try to get out of bed if they did not placate him, even if they did not understand his fear. They relayed his words to Gizur and one of the Canons visiting from Thykkvibær, who reflected, "He is quoting Hugh of St. Victor." Gizur assured the men he would clarify at once what Thorlák needed.

"Gizur!" The bishop greeted his closest advisor with urgency. "You must summon to me any whom I have excommunicated who are not yet reconciled. I must commute their sentences. I must permit them full access to sacramental life. I cannot leave them in a state of limbo."

Gizur set out immediately to honor his wish. Within two days, the men were found and brought to Skálholt. Thorlák was roused, given drink, and positioned so that he was resting comfortably upright. The men assembled in file around the bishop's sickbed, and he began to speak.

"My fellow countrymen," he began, pausing to breathe. "As your Shepherd, who prays for you day and night, excommunication pierces my heart with a wound I cannot bear."

He grimaced, gestured for a sip of water, and, clearing his throat, continued.

"Therefore, as your spiritual father, I invite you back into the flock of the faithful. I rescind my decree of excommunication and absolve you of your sins, imploring you in the words of Our Lord to go, and sin no more. *Í nafni Föðurins og Sonarins og hins Heilaga Anda…*"

Bishop Thorlák's pastoral blessing was interrupted.

The sound of poorly muffled laughter grew, like a swell, and crested in an unsuppressed cackle.

"He was wrong!" came the words. "Thorlák the Almighty just admitted he was wrong!"

Within a moment the other men were laughing too, and the heckling spread throughout the group.

"He says this from his deathbed to make us feel like he is doing us a favor!"

"This proves his threats are meaningless!"

"He knows we did nothing wrong and does not want to be remembered as a liar!"

"It is true what they say – he is an imbecile!"

The taunts continued until Gizur and another priest demanded silence from the miscreants. Thorlák closed his eyes, withstanding their insults as one unprepared takes sleet to the face in a sudden squall. He did not speak again until the melee had subsided, and when he did, his voice was small but firm.

"I decree that all my prior pronouncements shall stand until each man here reconciles himself with the penances I previously ordained, or else each shall await the verdict of the bishop who succeeds me."

He ordered the men be dispersed and he sunk backward into his pillow, pale and exhausted. He did not speak to anyone else for the remainder of that day.

CHAPTER TWENTY FOUR

THORLÁK'S FINAL DAYS

The decline of Thorlák's health came in spurts rather than a gradual conclusion. There were some days he seemed to sleep continuously, and others when he was alert and fretful about the affairs he wished to address in the time he could. Waking or sleeping, the stream of visitors seemed endless, and the bishop did what he could to receive each person with as much care as he could muster.

The immediate questions about his personal property concerned his associates much more than it did him. Thorlák allocated most of his belongings to the one who would succeed him in office. He apportioned money to his relatives and gifts to those he frequently invited to his residence. The two items of highest value were his rings: one, a gold ring which he bequeathed to Bishop Brand of Hólar, and the other, his consecration ring, which he set aside until he could speak with Páll.

"*Sonur minn*," Thorlák said to his nephew. "Do you know why I give this to you?"

Páll answered, "For me, it is the bare fact that I will

think of you and your words each and every time I gaze upon it. I will remember your striving to be the man worthy of this office."

"Yes, my Páll. Know me for who I am." Thorlák was weak and could not speak in any greater length.

Gizur Hallsson stayed by Thorlák's side night and day, telling him stories and reading from the Divine Office and St. Paul's letter to the Romans. Thorlák stopped him at intervals attempting to comment, sometimes forming words and other times murmuring too low to be understood. When Gizur reached chapter 3, verse 23 of the Letter to the Romans, Thorlák held up his hand.

"Read that again, my friend?"

"For all have sinned and fall short of the glory of God."

"I have sinned," said Thorlák, clearly and coherently. "I have been a difficult person to work with. I have been headstrong, and absorbed in my own thoughts. I have been harsh, unyielding… maybe I have not taken the time to know my fellow people in their weaknesses. Forgive me," he said. "Forgive me if I have done anything to you of which you did not think well."

Gizur embraced his bishop. "We should ask you that you forgive us for the things we have done amiss to you, which must be weighty and mighty!"

Thorlák promised in that instant that he held no ill feelings or retained any errors committed against him. Gizur, emboldened, implored: "Although you are now parting from us visibly in bodily presence, we pray, be to us a spiritual father, interceding for mercy with Almighty God – for we firmly believe that in the spiritual life, you will have no less power with God than now!"

Thorlák did not answer. He held Gizur's gaze for a long time, conveying more love in that prolonged moment than ever could have been spoken. Those present saw the tenderness and began to cry. Thorlák closed his eyes again, but then spoke to all gathered in his room: "Do not grieve, though our living together is interrupted, for I go according to my destiny. I have always been capable of little if others had not helped me. I am little loss to you, since after me will come a great leader. I comfort you in this, that I think I know certainly that God will not adjudge me a man doomed to hell."

Thorlák summoned and kissed each priest keeping

vigil in his room. He was anointed once more with Extreme Unction and positioned afresh. After that, he slept.

For seven days, Thorlák was half-conscious. Those keeping watch observed his lips moving and his expression changing, but he never fully awakened. If he could have been asked, Thorlák would have truthfully answered that he was experiencing wakeful visions. He was confident he was not asleep, as he was aware of everything and everyone in his surroundings… yet he was somehow able to see into the unseen, and respond with his intellect.

The first visions were dreadful. He found himself in the far west of Iceland near Gunnuhver (or, so he thought), where the ground gives way to sinkholes of boiling mud. The odor was like nothing he had ever smelled: a combination of fungus and decaying flesh, with the putrid stench of sulfur making it almost unbearable. As he peered toward the hot spots, he felt waves of distortion in his mind and heard guttural voices in his thoughts. "Thorlák… DEPART… be gone… away with you, at last, at last!" He shuddered and, in his mind, made the sign of the cross. He found himself in a desolate, gray place, at the foot of a basalt formation on a black sand beach. He was at Reynisfjara, on the south coast, and felt inconsolably alone. He began, in his mind, to speak to God.

"*Faðir*," he began, "I pray I have served You as You would have wished. I beg Your mercy on all whose lives have touched mine, from even before I was aware."

In his mind, he began to cry, but continued his prayer. "*Faðir*, You tell us, unless we acquire a heart like a child, we shall not enter Your Kingdom. But now –" He paused, sobbing. "Now, I fear I will not be admissible unto Your kingdom. For, as I reflect upon my life, I do not know when it was that I was ever a child. My search for You led me straight to the company of adults. I have worked so diligently to please my elders… to please You… that I have neglected my childhood! Oh, *Himneskur Faðir*, forgive me, forgive me!" He could not continue for the sobs convulsing his heart.

As he wept, he saw scenes from his life, both formative and ordinary. He saw the people smiling each time he passed. He was strangely, simultaneously, himself now, yet also in the third person, as others saw him… and he was filled with the same sensation he felt every time he performed a baptism.

"You were My child to each one who knew you, Elskan Minn," he heard in his mind. *"You taught them that childhood is not something you have once, and then lose… it is something you grow into as you come to know Me more and more. Now, if you are ready, come at last into the fullness of your childhood."*

Thorlák gasped incredulously. The beach disappeared and gave way to a field, an endless field of wild daisies, as far as he could behold. The sun shone warmly on them and the wind tickled them playfully, as if inviting him forward.

For the first time in years, he broke out in laughter. It bubbled, first a little, then more, then an uncontrollable fountain of joy, which in his mind sounded like the mirth of a young child.

He inhaled as deeply as he could, and ran, with full abandon, toward the field.

Suddenly he was roused by his advisors, who were discussing his care. Looking about, and coming to his senses, he felt uncomfortable and unkempt. He asked if he might have a change of clothing.

Startled by the lucidness of their dying bishop, the priests warned that attempting to move him would bring great discomfort. He quipped without missing a beat, "I hope for mercy from God from my anointing, not from these clothes." At that, he nodded sternly… and then, smiled. His advisors, completely disarmed, stammered their agreement and set out to accommodate his wish. None could believe they had been witness to Bishop Thorlák's first ever display of humor.

It was indeed arduous to help him into new clothing, but it was done, and fresh linens were placed on his bed. He rested once more, listening to Gizur read and sing the Divine Office, and felt a certain faintness overtake him.

"Where has Thorkell gone now?" asked Thorlák.

Thorkell Geirason, Thorlák's patron and brother in the Augustinian order, had died six years prior, almost as if to prepare a way for his mentor in the pattern of six, now in the afterlife. Gizur wondered at this question, but before he could answer, noticed Thorlák had ceased breathing.

Bishop Thorlák Thorhallsson died the evening before Christmas Eve, December 23, 1193.

CHAPTER TWENTY FIVE

EULOGY AND EPILOGUE

The body of Bishop Thorlák was carried into the cathedral and kept for three nights as the feast of Christmas was celebrated in solemn and somber tones. He was buried in the ground at Skálholt alongside the grave of the friend he cared for in his leprous last days. Many were present at Thorlák's burial. Gizur Hallsson preached the eulogy:

"It is good to remember the witness of our ancestors about those bishops who lived before our time, since the one whom they know best seems best to everyone. As glorious men as they were in their episcopates, the dignity with which Thorlák lived as bishop far surpasses all others. He was chaste all his life; well-mannered and virtuous; liberal and just; merciful and wise of counsel; humble but strict; meek of temper, with true love and affection for both God and men. He took consecration as a child, and the wisest men decided to increase his honor and consecration throughout his career. Even at a young age he placed himself under the holy Rule and maintained it right until death.

"Now, although it is commanded we must not predict the condition of a man after his death, there are few with any prospect of salvation if he is not full of bliss, as remarkable as Thorlák was in his life and good customs."

A letter received at a later date by now-Archbishop Eirik of Niðaros expressed his condolences thusly: "Our excellent brother, Bishop Thorlák, of fine memory, we believe has been holy in his life, but is now a glorious gemstone of power before God and of great authority."

Iceland, already accustomed to the long sleep of winter, slept more quietly than usual as 1194 arrived. Many reported dreaming of Bishop Thorlák. Indeed, Iceland itself seemed to sleep so it could dream of its boy hero, whose memory proved to be deeply imprinted in the hearts of the people he loved for centuries to come.

****

The grand ceremony was almost set to begin. Bishop Páll Jónsson, forty years of age and three years into his episcopate, managed to find a place where he could not be seen by the crowd outside the cathedral. There were more details than he could possibly attend to in this moment, but he deliberately removed himself for what he considered the most crucial preparation of the day.

Páll knelt on the ground next to his uncle Thorlák's gravesite and kissed the top. He raised his head and beheld the bell tower, the tallest structure in all of Iceland and easily its finest piece of workmanship. The construction, the crafting, the bells and their adornment had cost an enormous amount of money – more than the value of most farms – and had taken many weeks of dedicated labor to complete. The chapel at the base of the tower was bedecked in jewels, gold, silver, stained glass, murals and tapestries of the finest artisans, and would later that day be dedicated as the shrine to the newly proclaimed Saint Thorlák Thorhallsson. The bells had been purchased by Páll himself in Norway, and had been tested until they resounded in exact and glorious harmony. The cathedral, too, was outlaid in newly commissioned books and tapestries.

All said, the expenditure for this shrine's dedication was unprecedented, causing Páll's integrity to be questioned by many. As it was, his appointment in 1194 by Bishop Brand of Hólar seemed dubious, given that he was not a priest and was compelled to accept the post most vigorously by his father. Bishop Thorlák's death polarized many against Jón Loftsson as people reflected regretfully (and with growing sympathy) upon the abusive treatment he had endured at Jón's instigation. Yet many argued Páll was a good choice as one who sought the middle ground between political and ecclesial interests. Páll initially resisted, maintaining his unsuitability and insisting there be someone of greater preparation. In the end, he accepted after hearing this plea from one of the Canons at Thykkvibær: "Who is there who knows with intimacy the heart and mind of our Thorlák? That man, wherever he may be, should be our next bishop."

With Thorlák's dying words seared into Páll's mind, he accepted the appointment without further hesitation.

Kneeling now at Thorlák's gravesite, Páll prayed: "*Heilagur Biskup Thorlák*, I beg your patronage upon us this day..."

He stopped.

Páll stared at the gravesite, disrupted during the exhuming of Thorlák's remains and investigation into the cause of his sainthood; now, an empty plot, smoothed over and enshrined as a memorial to his uncle's death.

"I do want them to know you," he said, candidly breaking into conversation with his uncle's memory. "How maddening, that people make up their minds before having the benefit of knowing you. They look at me now and say I have done all of this to exalt my own position as bishop and chieftain. They look at me," he said, "as I once looked on your ring."

Páll held that very ring in the palm of his gloved hand.

"Today, I will do my best to show them who you really are. Please, *Frændi*... help me do so."

Unexpectedly, overhead, the bells tolled without announcement or preparation. Páll jumped to his feet. From behind the wall, he heard one of the priests shout, *"Fyrirgefðu!"* and realized it was the result of an overzealous brother wishing to ensure all was working properly.

Páll smiled. The festivities would begin shortly and he knew he needed to return to his station. As he went, he felt an inexplicable sense of peace, as though he were being reassured by an unseen hand, promising him:

I am always with you!

BIBLIOGRAPHY

Bagge, S. & Nordeide, S.W. Christianization and the Rise of Christian Monarchy: Scandinavia, Central Europe and Russia, c. 900-1200 Cambridge University Press: 2007

Basset, C. (trans.) Hungrvaka. Háskoli Íslands: 2013.

Brown, N.M. Song of the Vikings: Snorri and the Making of Norse Myths. St. Martin's Griffin, New York: 2014.

Brown, N.M. Ivory Vikings: The Mystery of the Most Famous Chessmen in the World and the Woman Who Made Them. St. Martin's Griffin, New York: 2015.

Cormack, M. The Saints in Iceland: Their Veneration from the Conversion to 1400. Société des Bollandistes, Brussels: 1994.

Dale, D. "The Early Bishops of Iceland." American Catholic Quarterly Review XLVI #184, 1921: pp. 529-555.

Emery, K. M. "Living on the Edge: Bioarchaeology of Medieval Iceland." September, 2015: http://bonesdontlie.wordpress.com

Feiss, H. A Companion to the Abbey of Saint Victor in Paris. Brill Academic Publishing: 2017.

Guðmundsson, G.F." Monasteries and Monasticism in Iceland During the Middle Ages." St. Ansgar's Bulletin, #93, 1997: pp. 15-19.

Guðmundsson, G.F. Þorlákur Helgi: The Life, Work and Influence of St. Thorlak, Patron Saint of the Icelandic People. Diocese of Reykjavík: 1998.

Guðmundsson, G.F. " Thorlak." St. Ansgar's Bulletin, #87, 1993: pp. 5-9.

Halborg, J.E. "Saint Thorlák Thorhallsson of Skálholt." St. Ansgar's Bulletin, #102. 2006: pp. 7-8.

Hugh of St-Victor, et al. On Love: A Selection of Works of Hugh, Adam, Achard, Richard, and Godfrey of St. Victor. Victorine Texts in Translation, Vol. 2. New City Press: 2012.

Jakobsson, Á. and Clark, D. The Saga of Bishop Thorlak. The Viking Society for Northern Research, University College, London: 2013.

Jensson, G. "The Lost Latin Literature of Medieval Iceland." Norwegian Journal of Greek and Latin Studies, Vol. 79, 2004: pp. 150-170.

Jensson, G. & Fahn, S.M. "The Forgotten Poem: A Latin Panegyric for St. Þorlákr in AM 382 4to. Gripla," 21 (2), 2010: pp. 19-60.

Johannesson, J. A History of The Old Icelandic Commonwealth: Íslendinga Saga. University of Manitoba Press: 2007.

Lacy, T. Ring of Seasons: Iceland, its Culture and History. University of Michigan: 2001.

Leffman, D. & Proctor, J. Rough Guide to Iceland. Rough Guides: 2016.

McCreesh, B. "Saint Making in Early Iceland." Scandinavian-Canadian Studies, Vol. 17, 2006-7: pp. 13-23.

Miller, W.I. "Some Aspects of Householding in the Medieval Icelandic Commonwealth." Continuity and Change 3 (3), 1988: pp. 321-355.

Rafnsson, S. "The Penitential of St. Thorlak in its Icelandic Context." Bulletin of Medieval Canon Law, New Series, Volume 15. Berkeley Institute of Medieval Studies: 1985, pp. 19-30.

Rafnsson, S. St. Thorlac: Patron Saint of Iceland. Diocese of Reykjavík: 1985.

Thurston, H.J. & Attwater, D. Butler's Lives of the Saints. Christian Classics, Westminster, MD: 1990, pp. 602-603.

Undset, S. "The Church in Iceland Prior to the Reformation." St. Ansgar's Bulletin, #40, 1942: pp. 1-5.

Undset, S. "A Saga of Greenland: The Ancestor of an Iceland Saint." St. Ansgar's Bulletin, #41, 1943: pp. 1-6.

Vesteinsson, O. The Christianization of Iceland: Priests, Power and Social Change, 1000-1300. Oxford University Press: 2000.

ABOUT THE AUTHOR

Aimee O'Connell is a wife, mother, certified school psychologist, and a person with Autism. She is also the founder of the Apostolate "The Mission of Saint Thorlák." And in her spare time (pun intended) she is also a fine researcher and writer.

"The Mission of Saint Thorlák" exists primarily to help those affected by Autism. Yet, as their website describes, the ministry is "for all hearts who hunger to be known for who they are (... that is to say, all hearts)."

As well as completing her first book, <u>Thorlák of Iceland: Who Rose Above Autism to Become Patron Saint of His People</u>, Aimee has recently had approved by the Catholic Church in Iceland a special Novena to Saint Thorlák.

Please visit "The Mission of Saint Thorlák" website for more information.

www.mission-of-saint-thorlak.com

www.ingramcontent.com/pod-product-compliance
Lightning Source LLC
Chambersburg PA
CBHW060012100426

42740CB00010B/1467